Monsieur Shoushana's Lemon Trees

PATRICIA DUNCKER was born in the West Indies. She teaches writing, literature and feminist theory at the University of Wales and lives for part of the year in France. *Hallucinating Foucault*, her first work of fiction, won Dillon's First Fiction Award 1996 and the McKitterick Prize for the best first novel published in 1996.

Also by Patricia Duncker

HALLUCINATING FOUCAULT

Monsieur Shoushana's Lemon Trees

PATRICIA DUNCKER

PICADOR

First published 1997 by Serpent's Tail

This edition published 1998 by Picador
an imprint of Macmillan Publishers Ltd
25 Eccleston Place, London SW1W 9NF
and Basingstoke

Associated companies throughout the world

ISBN 0 330 37113 4

1 3 5 7 9 8 6 4 2

A CIP catalogue record for this book is available
from the British Library.

Printed and bound in Great Britain by
Mackays of Chatham plc, Chatham, Kent

Contents

For S. J. D.

Frühling 1938

Heute, Ostersonntag früh
Ging plötzlicher Schneesturm über die Insel.
Zwischen den grünenden Hecken lag Schnee. Mein junger
  Sohn
Holte mich zu einem Aprikosenbäumchen an der
  Hausmauer
Von einem Vers weg in dem ich auf diejenigen mit dem
  Finger deutete
Die einen Krieg vorbereiteten, der
Den Kontinent, diese Insel, mein Volk, meine Familie und
  mich
Vertilgen mag. Schweigend
Legten wir einen Sack
Über den frierenden Baum.

Spring 1938

Today, Easter Sunday early morning,
A sudden snowstorm passed over the island.
Snow lay between the greening hedges. My young son
Brought me to a small apricot tree by the house wall,
Took me away from a verse in which I pointed the finger
At those preparing a war, which
May destroy the continent, this island, my people, my family
  and me.
Silently
We laid a sack
Over the freezing tree.

Bertolt Brecht
Translated by Patricia Duncker

Acknowledgements

These short stories were all written in France, where I have lived, more or less continuously, since the summer of 1986. The germ of each story was suggested to me by an event, person, conversation, or by a place that I know well. Apart from "The Glass Porch", which was set in Wales, and those stories that inhabit an entirely fictional space, the stories are all set in France.

I decided to let the people who share my life spend a little time in my fiction. So some acknowledgements are due. Thank you to Brigitte Boucheron, Sylviane Francesconi, Nadine Laroche, James Read, Gilles Roquelaure, Monsieur Guy Rousseau, Monsieur Franck Delhoume, Chantal Tascher, Fatima El Moussali, Nicole Thouvenot, Jacqueline Martel, Monsieur and Madame Pougeard, Monsieur le Directeur de l'Institut Universitaire de Technologie, Angoulême, Bernard Villechaise, for going on talking without noticing that I was taking notes – and the woman alone, wherever she is now. The totalitarian state in "The Storm" was invented with the political assistance of Peter Lambert. He also gave me advice on translating Brecht. Anne Jacobs is the woman without whom my life would be a grey place with too little laughter. S.J.D, to whom this book is dedicated, remains, as always, my first reader. Above all, thank you to the real Monsieur Shoushana for all his kindness and his lemon trees, and to my niece, the original Miranda.

"James Miranda Barry" was published in *The Pied Piper* edited by Anna Livia and Lilian Mohin (Onlywomen Press, 1989), "The Stations of the Cross" was first published in French as "Le Chemin de Croix" translated by Catherine Mahé, in *Lesbia Magazine* No. 100, December 1991, and in

English in *Feminist Studies* 20, No. 1, Spring 1994. "Betrayal" was published in *Sinister Wisdom* No. 46, April 1992, "The Glass Porch" appeared in *Luminous and Forlorn: contemporary short stories by women from Wales*, edited by Elin ap Hywel (Honno, 1994) and "The Crew from M6" first appeared in *Critical Quarterly* Vol. 38, No. 3, 1996. "The River and the Red Spring Moon" was published in *Stand Magazine* Vol. 37, No. 2, Spring 1996, "Aria Nova" in *Stand Magazine* Vol. 39, No. 1, Spring 1997, "The Arrival Matters" was published in *Insides Out: A Trio* (Kings Estate Press, USA, 1997) with two other novellas by Susan Dodd and Ruth Moon Kempher. I would like to thank the respective editors and publishers.

Patricia Duncker
France, 1997

Monsieur Shoushana's
Lemon Trees

It was dark and raining outside. I turned to leave the station, pushing my way through the crowd, when I heard someone calling my name. I turned to see one of my former students, Etienne, soaked through and carrying a small sack. He explained that he had hitchhiked all the way from Orléans and had arrived at Ruffec only to find that there were no more trains to Angoulême that night. The request never had to be voiced. I told him to get into the car. It was a long, dark drive south in thickening rain. So I asked him where he had been and he told me that he was working near Orléans, in an arms factory.

"It's not too bad. Only two months. We make bombs. Yes, missiles. Like the ones on television that are being used in the war. I'm working on fuses. Nowadays, it's all controlled by computer so there's a lot of electronics. We can't smoke. Obviously. We have to go a long way away to the canteen to smoke. There's lots of space. The factory is in a security zone, so that when you arrive, even if the guard knows you, you have to go through all the security checks. Every day it's the same. The buildings are huge. Just vast warehouses really. We wear white overalls and hats as if it was a hospital. We don't do nuclear warheads. Just conventional explosives. But some of them are fire bombs. And because the factory is potentially so dangerous there's lots of land around it that isn't used for anything. So we go hunting after work. Rabbits, grouse, pheasants, pigeons . . . There aren't any large trees except at the perimeter fence. It's all gorse, bush, undergrowth. There's a lake and a marsh rimmed with flags. We have a small flat-bottomed boat that we use for fishing. But I don't go in for that. Some people who've worked there for years know every corner. At the moment we're stepping up production. Because of the war. So there's not much time to hunt . . .

"Look. There's a lorry pulling out of the car park. He's bound to be going south. I'll hitch with him. Then you don't have to go so far out of your way. Thanks a lot. Goodnight. Goodnight."

I sat down at a table in the photocopying room where Chantal was programming the machine to print double-sided copies. I asked her what she was doing that weekend and she told me that they were taking the caravan to Royan.

"It's a campsite right by the sea, which Leroy Somer bought for their employees some years ago. Other people use it too, but we get reduced rates as members of the firm. For May and June it only costs fifty francs a week. Nothing at all really. We pay extra for electricity, but even then we get a better rate than the other visitors. We go out for weekends. Our friends have the site next door. Evenings we often have a barbecue. Sometimes the girls go there on their own to have a bit of a night out together at Royan. There aren't any main roads to cross to get to the sea. Just a small bicycle path and then the beach . . .

"No. We don't stay there in August. We take the caravan down to another site in the Midi. It's run by a Dutch couple. Lots of Dutch people go there, so they must advertise in Holland. It's about ten kilometres from Alès, near Nîmes, but that bit further inland. Sometimes it's hotter there than it would be at sea-level. But we're right by the River Gardon. I can bathe whenever I want. They haven't had so many book-ings since the war began, so we're sure to have our place next to the river, like last year. We only use the car once a week to go to the supermarket, otherwise we shop in the village. Just three kilometres away. We go on foot or on the bikes. It's so beautiful. A little Provençal village. With greenery all round the river and the red rocks above. Last year Delphine insisted that we go to Nîmes to see all the Gallo-Roman remains. Do you know the Arena? Yes, all that. They still use it for bull-fights. Well, it was 55 degrees in the car. I'm not joking. We'd have been better off staying home by the caravan. Oh, and there's something else that you must see – the Bambouserie. It's a bamboo plantation. Lots of different sorts. You'd think that you were in Asia. There are some giant bamboos with trunks this big. And you know, bamboo grows at a metre a day. Some of them do anyway. You can sit and watch. You even think that you can hear it grow. Yes, it's very near Alès. The man who planted the garden used to live in Asia – Indochina – I think. He had to come back because of some other war. And he brought back all these exotic species, which will grow in the Midi. Now his farm is engulfed by bamboo. Let me write down the address. No, next week I'll bring you their publicity brochure. I think that we've got one at home in the caravan. We'll have to clean it out before we take it over to Royan. And the photographs we took last year. I'll bring them in to show you. *Allez, à la semaine prochaine!*"

I walked down the road in the dusk to the house by the river. Here we drank coffee and Benedictines with Monsieur Shoushana, who has another home in Nice. I asked him if he had a garden there and he told me that he had the most beautiful lemon trees.

"Ah, yes. Two wonderful lemon trees. Just below the terrace. Do you know the blossoms? The most lovely blossoms. There are several hectares at the back of the house where we grow mandarins and blood oranges. I keep the grass very short and rough. We sell them to a vendor in the market. Yes, I make a little money on the side. There's been panic buying in Nice since the war started. Crazy, isn't it? The economy in France isn't affected. We concentrate on the orange trees for fruit to sell. But at ten, eleven o'clock at night, we sit out on the terrace and I can see the lemons gleaming in the dark. Do you know Nice? It's a beautiful city. The English have always loved Nice. In the nineteenth century they went there to die. Yes, they have their own church and their own library. Their own cemetery, too. We very rarely have any snow in the winter. There was one bad year when we had a lot of frost and a snowstorm. It lasted a week. Most unusual. They had to replace some of the palm trees, which had frozen to death. I covered my lemon trees with plastic sheeting and they survived. Not so many lemons that year, but just as many the next. One day you must come to Nice and see my lemon trees."

I was looking at official documents in Fatima's flat when the doorbell rang. It was her friend Djabar. He took off his boots at the door, as I had done, and came in cautiously. He sat down in the rocking chair and looked at the damp toes of his socks. I asked him if he had any news. And he told me that he had no news.

"My family rang on the night of January the fifteenth. When the war was finally declared they rang me up. And they got through that night to say goodbye. Since then I have had no news."

And he said nothing more.

The Stations of the Cross

The interview had been appalling. We were all requested to be there at 9 a.m. and there we were at twenty to nine in a nervous self-conscious row, looking at our knees. The committee turned up an hour later and walked in and out of the room fingering their files, chatting to each other and ignoring us. Finally, a well-dressed block of masculinity with the eyes of an assassin told us in what order we would be called. Then he went back inside the committee room and shut the door. We sat awaiting judgement in a windowless green corridor. The Spanish candidate and the solitary, bright-eyed young woman who was the only candidate for Polynesian languages all pushed off, gossiping and clutching plastic coffee cups. The candidate next to me was a mother of two, who had written a thesis on Karen Blixen and the images on the covers of books. She was Danish, married to a Frenchman and ran a private school in Antibes, which had just gone bankrupt. Hence, her application.

She seemed so unlikely that I kept looking at her hair and lipstick. Her hair was blond turning grey, and her lipstick was bright red. The third candidate was a sinister American with a moustache who kept crossing and uncrossing his legs and looking at us out of the corner of his eye. We waited for another twenty minutes, engaged in uneasy, twittering conversation. I asked questions, on the offensive. The others talked away, revealing all, as some travellers do on planes.

Then the brute re-emerged from the committee room and called me.

The next twenty minutes were harrowing. He had read every word of the writing I had sent in. And had written down his own list of searching questions, any one of which I would have evaded, twisted, reformulated or challenged had they arisen in the course of an intimate conversation with someone I had known for thirty years. The other members of the committee, all men, apart from an eerie character dressed up as Snow White's stepmother, began to be puzzled by his peculiar line of questioning and my tortuousness.

The wicked queen decided to intervene and put all the cards straight on the table.

"Have you applied for this post as a way of insinuating yourself into the education system?" she asked maliciously.

The brute turned on her unexpectedly. "Don't be silly. That's never occurred to her."

And indeed, it hadn't.

He gazed at me for a moment. I had now begun to answer in monosyllables.

"I imagine," he said speculatively, "that you would go there with every intention of staying for ever."

"Yes," I said.

He pounced. "Have you applied to any universities in Britain?"

"No."

"Or in Germany?"

"No."

Pause.

"I don't understand. Why aren't you part of your professor's harem?" He had turned nasty.

"I'm just not."

Now everyone was baffled.

He gave up. "Thank you." He looked down at his papers. I was dismissed.

So I fled away to a bar-pizzeria covered in pink pictures of antique cars and burst into tears. My black stockings itched, the high heels pinched, I hadn't worn the dress for over a year and the lace collar now filled me with loathing. I had turned up well-disguised, prepared to engage in the little game of keen, arse-licking careerist, and had walked into a trap. For the first time in my life the enemy had carefully read every word of my secret dispatches and tried to decode them. Failing to do so, he had smelt subversion.

I thought I was going to be sick.

"*Qu'est-ce que vous prenez, Madame?*" The voice was carefully arranged so that the question was different, but unmistakable.

"What can I give you that will stop you crying?"

"*Un café.*"

A cognac arrived with the *café.*

Two huge ugly men, one at the bar, one behind it, nodded at me encouragingly. I looked at my red, swollen face emerging from a sodden Kleenex in the bar mirror and knew every one of my forty years. I sniffed miserably into the cognac. When I could speak I asked him if he had a telephone.

"We don't have a telephone. But there's one opposite." He pumped out sympathy like a steam turbine. "I can sell you a card if you like."

I already had one, but I bought another to thank him for the cognac. I left my blue notebook and pencil in the café and battled with the phone box. I rang Brigitte.

"How did it go?" she demanded.

"Awful. I hated them and they hated me."

"Oh, no. What did they say?"

"They as good as accused me of being a dangerous revolutionary with a knife between my teeth."

"I thought you were wearing a dress."

"And stockings. And high heels." I sniffed into the phone.

"Come back at once, *ma grande,*" said Brigitte, all solicitude.

Years of unemployment and misery as an embittered intellectual stretched before me. I rang Nadine.

"Everything's fine," she said, "except the chain saw. It just cut out."

I imagined the alternatives: an enormous bill, or hours sharpening the axe.

"Don't worry," I said, "it's probably the security device."

"How did it go?" she asked.

I started crying again into the receiver.

"Why didn't you wear a dress?" demanded Nadine.

Sympathy in the café had increased tenfold. They had been counting my Kleenex consumption in the phone box. I paid, gathered up my books and escaped from the devastating waves of caring support.

"*Bon courage, Madame!*" they chanted like Verdi's chorus.

I got into the car and drove out of the city as fast as I could. My mind emptied out into a meaningless screen like the television test card. I saw the huge arc of trees above the straight road, the dry earth blowing dust at the foot of the vines, and the warm red houses, their blinds already down against the midday sun. I registered nothing. A little bridge, a slight incline, the road began to rise towards the red mountains. I slowed down and as I did so I started shaking with wretchedness, humiliation and resentment. My black stockings prickled in the heat.

I looked up.

High above me on a red rock ridge I saw a row of little chapels, each one surmounted by the cross, equidistant from one another, their lead roofs shiny in the sun. There were fourteen, not quite facing each other, so that I could see the back of one and the wrought-iron doorway of the other opposite. As I came closer the angle changed and I could only see a row of red roofs and crosses. At the end of this religious cavalcade was a slightly larger chapel, no doubt containing a grisly plaster-cast effigy of the Crucifixion.

These were the stations of the cross.

At the foot of the red rock ridge decorated with faith there was a lay-by. I pulled in and stopped. At the foot of the cross

I sat down and wept. I wept into the ashtray, I wept onto the dashboard, I wept over the steering-wheel. I wept until my face was scarlet and swollen. I wept for all my failures, for all the lies that I had ever told, for all the illusions in which I had believed, and for all the times I had pretended to be something other than the person that I am. I drank down the whole cup of bitterness in the garden of red rocks.

And then I realized that I was sitting in chains. I leapt out of the car, threw open the boot and searched for my T-shirt and jeans. I stamped the high heels under foot, peeled off the stockings, flung the dress into my black sack. Wearing nothing but knickers, feeling the sun warming my back, bare feet on warm asphalt, and the wind drying my tears, I stretched my arms high above my head and began shouting; long, exhilarating, joyous shouts which only come to the women who take off their stockings and high heels.

Then a little grey Citroën with a man in it pulled into the lay-by.

I stopped shouting and pulled on the T-shirt. The jack was loose in the boot of the car. I clasped its oily handle grimly and prepared to scatter his brains at the foot of the cross if he took one single step towards me. The man hastily looked the other way and pulled up further ahead of me. He got out of his car. I fingered the jack. He opened his boot and took out three large grey boxes, not very deep, with a grille round the rim. He lifted each one carefully, keeping them level. He laid them out in a row. The boxes vibrated slightly. Fascinated, clutching the jack, I circled the car.

He opened the boxes, one after another, and there arose into the sky a giant flood of a hundred pigeons. They wheeled upwards in a great curve, a whirring, churning mass of grey and blue wings, rising, striding the warm wind. Then swung outwards in elegant formation, high above the iron cross of the Crucifixion. The arc of birds widened and finally vanished into the deepening, endless blue.

Betrayal

Hélène held a dinner party to which she invited all her ex-lovers. Her most recent ex-lovers. I was the only person there who hadn't been to bed with her. Unfortunately, I was late. Thus, when I arrived, there were three faces shimmering with jealousy, arranged around the table. The post of Hélène's lover, usually occupied by at least two women who were never allowed to meet, theoretically out of respect for both but in fact to avoid broken crockery and nasty scenes, was currently held on short-term renewable contract by a ravishingly beautiful ballet dancer with supple encircling arms and a back like a concrete curtain wall. She was hindering Hélène's cooking by administering torrents of kisses. The three other women watched, furious.

"Hello everyone," I cried, realizing that the only lover I knew was the ballet dancer.

I tried to create an amiable diversion. I was the only person not close to an outburst of hysterical murderousness. I unloaded my box. I was carrying alcohol, oranges and eggs. All the different colours looked charming on the table. Everyone smiled and clapped. The tension ebbed.

"Do you know Louise?" accused one of the jealous faces as the ballet dancer coiled herself around me.

"Oh yes, we've met," I said cautiously.

"Today is my birthday. I can do anything," cried Louise and involved herself sexually with casseroles and cooking pots.

I sat down to look at the row of ex-lovers. One was very

fat, one was very thin and one was very small. I decided that I was under an obligation to become an ex-lover as I am very tall, in order to complete the row. They were all creative, interesting women, their faces twisted with jealousy. Louise made love to the herrings, then we got two each, bristling with butter and parsley. Hélène enjoyed every moment of our discomfort.

"And how is Anna?" asked one of the ex-lovers, suddenly turning very nasty as we melted our square sugars in tiny cups. Anna is the most beautiful woman I have ever seen. Anna is Hélène's other lover. Anna has tenure in the post.

"Ah . . . *ça va*," said Hélène uneasily. Louise rumbled like Etna. All the ex-lovers looked pleased. Hélène and I looked at each other shiftily, like suspected conspirators.

The ex-lovers pushed off at midnight. I discovered that they were all staying together like the three musketeers. Louise was dancing in front of the mirror in the bathroom. Hélène and I smoked at the bottom of the garden. Her city seems unlighted in the night; the only spotlit monument is the cathedral, a massive red-brick fortress in which the local Protestants were massacred. It is full of famous fifteenth-century sculptures attributed to an Italian master of Giotto's school. All the women look shifty, with ambiguous eyes. The Magdalens cover their pots, the Virgins pull their robes around them, Judith is no better than she ought to be. Hélène loves the cathedral. This is entirely suitable.

We watched the red turrets burning in the warm night. It was my serve.

"Hélène, I know that this is going to sound silly as you obviously had a scenario of some kind in mind. But why on earth did you invite them all on the same evening?"

She stared at me resentfully, like a child being bullied. "Chantal did that to me. Invited all her ex-lovers. And they were all friends. Friends! Can you imagine? They got on. And I was the only woman there who was a cauldron of jealousy. I thought I'd explode."

I looked at her. I was about to say something patronizing and brutal about petty vendettas and revenges that ruined good dinners. But I thought better of it and smiled wearily. "Let's have a beer," I said.

I have never been in love with Hélène, but I am very fond of her.

Do heterosexual people permit themselves the luxury of breaking up, then hating each other for ever – with impunity? Do they just vanish into that great safe sea of other heterosexuals and never see one another again? Martin tells me that gay men sometimes never know who it is that they have just sucked off. I said that it must be odd to kiss only cocks, not faces. He said that he liked the mystery and that cocks were often more honest than faces. And then again, I do know gay men, Martin among them, who have devastating love affairs, every bit as horrendous as our own, and storm out of rooms, smashing glasses against potted plants. I have seen poets pinned against radiators, facing accusations of infamy which revealed the Tolstoyan dimensions of the accuser's imagination. Or perhaps the astonishing sexual talents of the accused. Jealousy magnifies, distorts, like a fairground mirror. It turns the lover and the beloved into monsters.

With us it is not possible to run away from the past. Your ex-lover is your present lover's ex-lover but one, which is when she was with you. And if you try to escape the enchanted castle by advertisements in another area you'll find that the woman who replies was lovers with your first lover after she was married and before she came out for real this time and hasn't she changed? The silk twist that binds us is unbreakable, invisible, eternal. It is like God's love: theoretical, ever-present and stifling. We meet what is actually just one of the facts of life in small communities with a barrage of ideologies – lesbian ethics, significant friendship and political continuity. Sometimes this works. As it did with Chantal's ex-lovers who all but formed a collective. More often it is simply a veil for resentment, insecurity, violence and hypocrisy. Real feeling, brutal but honest, is channelled into decent behaviour in a fashion worthy of an English village church flower committee. Mind you, I'm not an enemy of decent behaviour and when I lived in an English village one of those nice tight-curled, blue-rinsed old ladies drove one of the others on the flower rota to a nervous breakdown. I told my mother all about it. "Oh yes," she said, "they're all lesbians."

Well, Hélène and Louise got up and went off to work the next morning. Not particularly early. I heard them making love in a welter of shrieks and cries. It sounded fun. I stroked the cat. She's an interesting cat. Multicoloured, and she dreams. God knows what about. Sometimes in the night she turns circles at the bottom of the bed, spitting and growling. Hélène told me that one rare night when she was sleeping alone she took the harlequin cat to bed with her. In the grip of a nightmare the cat bit her ear and she had to have an anti-tetanus injection. "How did you do that?" asked the doctor. "My cat bit me in her dreams," said Hélène and the doctor went away shaking his head. "You could put an earring through it," I suggested.

I walked round the town. It was quiet, sunny and free of tourists. The British and the Dutch arrive in July. By the time they get this far south they've already caught the sun. The British have become pink shrimps with densely packed freckles. The Dutch are a magnificent toasted brown. The British have thermos flasks and are carrying melted plastic sacs of freezing fluid for their picnic boxes. The Dutch wear anti-nuclear T-shirts and new trainers. I watch them going into their hotels. This time of year the terrace under the cathedral is empty. So I sat down with a coffee, my blue note book and a sense of well-being. I was still writing when Hélène's Mercedes cruised round the corner.

Hélène is not rich. She inherited a bit of money last year, but she spent that on a laser photocopier and a new computer. She's always had the Mercedes. It's one of those 1968 models with fins, leather seats and a walnut dashboard. She loves it so much that I always say it's her other lover. The third lover, who is never in danger of becoming her ex-lover. She's put in seat belts, even at the back, and she has a mechanic who loves it as much as she does. Early in the spring she got all the rust done and gave it a respray. It's the original colour now – luxurious, strokeable cream.

"Get in quick," said Hélène, "we'll pick up Louise."

"Where are we going?"

"The Conquistadora. You wanted to see everyone, didn't you?"

"Hélène. Do you know what you're doing?"

"Of course I do. It's all arranged."

Anna runs the Conquistadora. With her ex-lover. The one before Hélène. Mine not to reason why. I felt like declaring that she could certainly do as she liked, but that I was just an ordinary person who poured acid on her verrucas every morning.

So we drove away across hills, past fields rampant with poppies, banks overflowing with wild daisies. The corn was rising fast in the May days. I cheered up as the Mercedes cruised over the hills like Aladdin's carpet. Sunk in leather and cushions, my feet on wool mats, it was like driving along in a private club. The sun laid little warm kisses all along my arm. Louise was doing the same thing to Hélène. Nobody had premonitions of disaster.

It's always exciting arriving in cities. Even the obligatory ten kilometres of horror, half-made roads, dank canals and pink-brick high-rise blocks were interesting. I looked around, enjoying the mixture of flash investment and decrepitude. The Conquistadora is a discreet private club in a back street. It's surprisingly light inside. They don't have a licence to sell hard liquor, but they do beer, coffee and cocktails. They serve food. The cook is Spanish and she's called Maria. Her food is worth fighting for and so is she. Anna says that Maria is courted with flowers every evening, by the woman she had chatted to the night before. She's employed to be nice to everyone. So everyone is in love with her. I once asked for her photograph. She gave me one from a stash she keeps under the bar. We were early. So only Maria and Anna's ex-lover were there. Both of them were cleaning glasses and smiling at each other.

I bought everyone a drink. Anna and her ex-lover are on Weight Watchers, so they only drink Vittel. Nobody here believes in learning to love their natural body weight. The dominant ideology, as seen on TV, says that we all have to be as thin as pencils; so we are. And if you aren't, you join Weight Watchers and diet. We were all pleasantly relaxed and the bar began to fill up at dusk. Then Anna walked in.

A woman who is brazen enough to hold an exclusively ex-lovers dinner party should not flinch when her two current lovers, both of whom are quite aware of the situation and who the other one is, actually, finally, eventually meet. Anna knew it wasn't me, so it had to be the other one. The tall one with the back like an engineering construction and the arms like fluid tentacles. Anna kissed me. Hélène slunk into a corner. Louise looked into her drink.

Anna is very, very beautiful. You'd think she's older than she is. She has black hair, cut like an Italian page boy, and wonderful brown eyes. She's the sort of woman who poisons your wine if you don't make love well, but covers you in roses if you do. She's tireless, dynamic, organized. Other women grow in her soil as if she were pure fertilizer. She stays close friends with all her ex-lovers.

"Well," she said, smiling at Hélène, "aren't you going to introduce me?"

Hélène hid guiltily under a table. And so it was I who introduced Anna to Louise. They kissed each other very cautiously, three times, one cheek after the other. Then they stepped back. Anna smiled. I told you, didn't I. Anna is the most beautiful woman I know. Louise thought so too. I could tell that she did. They liked each other. That was dreadful, it really was adding irony to injury. And so the evening began.

In some ways it went well. Maria's food was spicy and peculiar. Anna's ex-lover was pleased with the situation, played soft music and was charming to her customers. All our friends came up to join us. We sat at a large table, argued about politics, the war, books, moaned about money and unemployment, gossiped about the past. We ordered more wine. Christelle came in at around ten o'clock. I abandoned my self-appointed post as amiable distraction to talk to her, just us, at another table.

"How's it going?" I asked her.

"Oh, fine. Really fine. I'm just starting my third year at the hospital and I'm off on a *stage* next Monday. Paediatrics. A hospital in the Pyrénées. Just three weeks. I'm looking forward to it. *Ça va me changer mes idées*. I've had a bit of a problem. No, not with Isabelle. She's not a lesbian, you know. She's straight. But she's still my best friend. Well, yes, at the beginning she had all the usual prejudices. She actually said that she couldn't stand lesbians. So I said, well, do you like me, *parce que moi, je suis comme ça*. I know it's taking a risk. But it worked. She was really shaken. She realized that she was quite wrong about women like us. And she didn't drop me. She started asking questions. We came here once. She really liked it. She liked the way that the women were all dressed up. And that we chatted about ordinary things. Funny, isn't it, the ideas people have. She did have a boyfriend, but it wasn't going too well with him. He wanted it all his own way; so she packed it in and told him to push off. Then suddenly, when I was round at her house, her parents – it was her mother at first – started in on me. Really nasty. Saying how I wasn't welcome there as I wasn't the kind of person they wanted to have around. But nothing explicit. Well, I went away at once and I wouldn't go into the house again. I just sound the horn at the gate and Isabelle comes out. I asked her what on earth had gone wrong as her parents had always been so sweet to me before. God, they've known me since the *sixième*. I've always been her best friend. And she said that she'd tackled her dad and he'd said that he wasn't born yesterday and he could see that I was *comme ça* and he didn't want his daughter being led astray by women like that. Is it written all over my face? Or my clothes? Do I look like a lesbian? What does a lesbian look like? We all look different, don't we? Was it that I didn't talk about boyfriends? Or bring one round? *Merde*, I had to tell Isabelle straight out. She's my very best friend and she hadn't noticed. So what's so special about her parents? My parents know. They accept it. But I wouldn't want my mother to hear people criticizing me in the street. Or getting phone calls. It's all caused problems for Isabelle. She won't drop me. She's too loyal. I know, I thought that too. And it's because of that honesty and courage that she's still my best friend. Even if she is straight. But she's quarrelled with her parents and she's very upset."

"Did her boyfriend know that you were a lesbian?" I asked. She looked astonished.

"Yes, he did. He must have done. I think Isabelle told him."

"Look no further than the ex-lover," I said.

Sometimes we betray each other unforgivably, giving away kingdoms, selling the pass to the enemy for a lot less than thirty pieces of silver. But sometimes we betray each other in tiny ways. Over very ordinary things.

All was not well within the eternal triangle. Anna had noticed something which she did not like. It was eleven o'clock and the room was full of smoke. The meal was over and tempers were bottoming out. The bar was overladen with women, leaning inwards like chickens over their millet dispenser. Someone chose very loud music. Louise got up to go to the loo and Anna immediately asked Hélène to step outside. A deadly hush, worthy of the moment when the saloon door swings open and the gunslinger walks in, descended over our table. But some little part of us was excited and delighted. We all turned white as daisies. Louise came out of the loo and saw at once that Anna, who had been looking dangerous, had gone. Nor was there any sign of Hélène.

"Let's dance," cried Louise, seizing my arm with her double-jointed tentacle. That was the signal, I suppose. The room suddenly erupted with pure joy. We waltzed, we tangoed, we smooched. We even did a Russian dance, bobbing about on our buttocks, flinging our legs out with maniacal enthusiasm. We menaced the floor-boards, thumping out splintering rhythms. The entire café-restaurant joined us. Someone started taking photographs. Someone mean bought two rounds of drinks and paid for them with a 500 franc note. Anna's ex-lover sellotaped it to the bar mirror as a trophy. We yelled for more wine. I must have given myself a hernia. Louise danced with every woman in the house, bewitching them all with her strength and grace. We clapped. We cheered. We wanted more. We were all young and in love. We didn't notice when Anna came back into the bar, her face silent and blank.

Exuberance subsided into stupor at about two o'clock. Louise and I waltzed down the street and stumbled into the glistening creamy Mercedes. Hélène was weeping over the steering wheel. Huge heart-rending sobs pouring over the upholstery.

We put the car into the *lavage* at Intermarché late next morning to wash away the trauma of the night. I stood beside Hélène watching the rainbow dervishes glitter and whirl. We were hollow-eyed, hung over and depressed. It was not a moment to bother with tact.

"So you didn't tell her you were still sleeping with Louise?" I said bluntly.

"How could I?"

"Well, you told her that you were still sleeping with that other woman last year, didn't you?"

"Of course. We have no secrets. It's very important to be utterly honest."

"I see."

"I would have told her."

"But she noticed before you had the chance to do so."

Hélène shrugged remorsefully. "I'm in a dreadful state," she said.

We stood watching her 1968 Mercedes becoming gradually whiter with foam.

A week later Hélène rang me up and said "Hello" in a very shaky voice.

"I've finished with Louise."

"Oh God, was it awful?"

"She shouted and cried and made a scene in the street."

"Did she come round to see you at the house?"

"Yes. Once. And Anna was there."

"Oh my God."

"Anna sat at the bottom of the garden while Louise blacked my eye. It's still yellow round the edges."

"Oh no," I groaned weakly, "she actually hit you."

"And then she came round the next morning to apologize and that was much worse. She sat on my lap for three hours and we both cried ourselves into hysterics. Then Chantal came past on her way to her judo lesson and she started crying too."

"Listen," I said, "don't go anywhere. I'm coming down to see you."

But Hélène's eye recovered its usual sensuous lustre and our community re-established its equilibrium. Louise still wasn't speaking to Hélène; and so we all waited patiently for Louise to get over it and come round. Wounded feelings are a luxury most of us are unable to afford. Pride is never a cheerful long-term companion. You get lonely after a while. But Louise didn't come round. Hélène sent her a little note. Louise sent it back. I sent her a card. Louise rang me up and said that she didn't feel like dancing any more. It's very hard being someone's ex-lover. We all are. But that doesn't make it any easier.

The days were getting colder when I pulled in at the petrol pump by the *lavage*. The boy on the pump looked at me hard, then lit up with instant recognition.

"It was you, wasn't it? Who put the car into the *lavage*. And left all the windows open."

"No. Not me."

But someone with a really nice old Mercedes had done it. Paid for a forty franc wash and had the *mousse* foaming all over the leather seats, hand-stitched cushions and into the shopping bags. She had stood there screaming as the water poured in through every pore, into the body of the car. Screaming, but powerless to stop the dancing rainbow whirls.

Only one person in town drove an elderly Mercedes. I walked thoughtfully down the cat food section, peering at cans of Gourmet and Sheba. Suddenly a woman's arm snaked around my waist and I abandoned my trolley in a waltz. Louise took the lead, guiding my steps, her eyes glittering like fencing rapiers. I hugged her and she laughed.

"You did it."

"I never did."

"You're dancing."

She smiled.

Death Before Dishonour

My first thought was that my wife must be having an affair. I'm not usually a jealous man but I've read all the books. I know the signs. What I should be looking out for: any change in her usual behaviour, new clothes, doing her hair differently, unexplained silences. Sometimes these things begin long before anything more serious happens; anything irrevocable, if you see what I mean. The first time I noticed anything odd was on the night she turned the lights off.

We have a small flat in the 18th, rue Ordener. There's a market in the road on Saturdays where she does all the shopping. That day she'd bought flowers, carnations, blood-red, which she put in the bedroom. She buys flowers every Saturday, but she usually puts them on the table. I asked her why she'd put them in the bedroom and she said that you could still see them from the sitting-room if the doors are open, and they always are. We've got fifty-two square metres all in all, counting the lobby, so we leave the bedroom doors open to make it feel a bit wider. It's a big apartment compared with the others in the block and the lavatory is separate from the bathroom; but it's narrow, two long narrow spaces side by side, and the kitchen is a slit along the living-room wall. There's only room for one in the kitchen. But she prefers being in charge. She keeps a firm hand on the fridge. Well, the day she put the carnations in the bedroom was the same day she turned the lights off.

Her mother and aunt had been round to supper. We had

entrecôte grillée cooked in that spicy sauce which her aunt loves, plenty of green pepper, nutmeg and *crème fraîche*. The usual family talk, her mother going on about the grand-children. We don't have any children; her sister has three. I've got a cold cupboard in the cellar and I'd fetched up a good Côtes de Bourg. They drank it all and I drove them home to Vitry around midnight. When I got back my wife had cleared up the flat, done the pots and was already in bed reading a Japanese thriller to the slow rumble of the dishwasher. The carnations glowed in the light from her bedside lamp. I talked to her a little while I was getting undressed. She didn't really reply, just murmured yes occasionally, but then, she was deep in her thriller. I got into bed and lay there thoughtfully. We've been married ten years, so I don't have to approach these things indirectly. I leaned over under the sheet and pulled her nightgown up over her knees. She didn't move, so I stroked the top of her left thigh. She went on reading for a while and then she did a quite extraordinary thing. Extraordinary for her, that is. She took off her glasses, put them in the book to mark her place and turned off the light.

Now I prefer to make make love with the light on. So that I can see what I'm doing. She's got a good body still for a woman her age. She's never had children so her stomach is firm; round, but firm. She's got large breasts with big, pink nipples. Like I say, I like to see what I've got underneath me. She wasn't saying that she didn't want to, because no sooner had she turned the light off than she turned to face me and pulled her nightgown right up to her chin. I didn't quite know what to say and the light's on her side. So I got on with it in a businesslike way to show that I wasn't put out. The streetlights come into the room anyway, producing an eerie half-light. But you don't notice them when the lamps are lit. I reached out and patted her head when I'd finished. I asked her why she'd turned off the light. She didn't say anything in reply. But I think that she was just going off to sleep.

Everything was normal the next day. She got up to make

the coffee at eight-thirty. She went out to the *boulangerie* in her slippers. She filled in her loto forms. She cleaned the bathroom after I'd had my shower. She was cooking again by eleven-thirty. I didn't exactly forget it, the business with the lights, but I put it away in the back of my mind.

Weekdays we usually leave the block together. I work in a garage out on the *périphérique*, near the Porte de Pantin. It's a good job, regular hours and a fair wage. I'm the head mechanic, so I have the responsibility of doing the estimates. I'm a cautious man and I don't take decisions quickly. I like to weigh things up. My wife never asks me about my work, but you don't expect women to be interested in cars, do you? She works with her sister on the Ile St-Louis. Her sister runs a hotel and my wife does the accounts; the reception in the summer and supervises the cleaning. Often as not she does the cleaning herself. Can't bear anyone else to do it half-heartedly so that it has to be done again. She uses savage-smelling products for which you are advised to wear gloves. They don't smell of pine and lavender, just disinfectant. And sometimes she does too. It's a very aggressive smell. I did speak to her about it once. She agreed to wear a stronger perfume if I found the smell unpleasant.

She eats lunch with her sister and in the winter she's always home before I am. In the summertime she does the hotel reception three evenings a week and gets home at eleven. She never does weekends. I always ask after her sister. She tells me about her sister's children. What they get up to. The oldest boy goes fishing in the river now, but they never eat anything he catches because the water's too polluted. He's made friends with an old chap on a barge and they fish in the afternoons. Daughter is just going into the *sixième* and the youngest is under their feet at the hotel all day during the summer. Her sister won't leave him in the *garderie*. She seems to be fond enough of her sister's children. She never forgets their birthdays. But she's not what I would call maternal. In the first years of our marriage I was roaring keen for babies. I wanted a son of my own. Only natural, that. But nothing happened. We went to the clinic and had all the tests and the counselling. They said that we just had to be patient. Nothing was wrong exactly. It just hadn't taken. By the time she'd turned forty we'd already given up thinking about it.

It was a month after the incident with the light that I got home around seven and she wasn't there. The flat was empty. Her bag wasn't there, her umbrella wasn't in the corner. She was late. I switched on the TV and watched the news. But it was past eight-thirty before I heard her key in the door. Must have been after eight-thirty because Laurent Cabrol was on, apologizing for the weather and showing us a *clin d'oeil* of hedgehogs doing a mating ritual.

I was a bit annoyed. So I didn't say anything; I went on with my beer and the beginning of the film. She apologized for being late, but she didn't give a reason. If she didn't want to tell me, that was her affair. But that night she switched off the light again just as I had made it clear that I fancied a bit of love. And she switched it off just a little too briskly.

I'm not usually a jealous man. But I'm not naïve. And I'm not easily taken in. I was now on the watch. Things went on as usual all that spring, but she wouldn't make love with the light on. It became something of a battle of wills. I decided to withdraw a little. I didn't ask her for sex. And she didn't come over for a cuddle like she used to. But nothing was said. If she didn't want to talk about it, then neither did I.

But she didn't seem to want to talk about anything. One evening I asked her where she'd like the caravan this year. We keep it in the yard at her mother's place in the suburbs. And every year we book a site somewhere on the west coast or in the Midi. I enjoy going through the brochures and working out which campsite is the best bargain. Anyway, she showed no interest in the brochures and said that she hadn't considered going on holiday this year. Wasn't sure she would. I must admit I did get a bit irritated by that. I suppose I shouldn't have shouted at her. She got up quietly and went straight to bed. And the next night she didn't come home until well after nine o'clock. I'd given up hope of supper and been down to the café. I took a piece of fish out of the freezer for her and left it thawing on the draining board. Like I say, I know I shouldn't have shouted at her, but she'd stopped being cooperative. I was all ready to apologize and make things all right again. But when I saw her I couldn't bring out a single word. She was dead white, like someone in shock after an accident and her hands were shaking. She said yes, she didn't feel too well, but would be all right in the morning, and no, she wouldn't eat anything but was going straight to bed. I thought I heard her retching over the basin, but she'd locked the bathroom door so I couldn't be sure.

She had great black circles under her eyes next morning, but she got up and went to work as usual. She didn't say much and she didn't put the breakfast plates in the dishwasher like she usually did. It was then that I knew. She was seeing someone else. And he was putting pressure on her.

I rang her sister next day after my wife would have left work and said I was worried. That she'd looked tired and ill, but that she kept saying that everything was all right. Now I'd thought that her sister would get all evasive, which would prove that she was in the know. But she didn't. Instead she got all het up and genuinely worried. I know the girl well and she wasn't shamming. She must have had a go at my wife because I was told to mind my own business the following evening when she came in. Late. She was still a bit white, but she had her chin in the air like a gladiator. Suit yourself, I thought. And something ended, then and there between us. Can't put my finger on it exactly, but it didn't make me happy. I wasn't in her confidence any more. She was silent.

And then she stopped coming home. She stopped making supper at least three nights a week. Sometimes she'd be back at nine, sometimes midnight. If I talked to her she answered in monosyllables. I decided to find out who the other man was before I made my final accusations.

I took a day off work. I followed her.

It was hard to keep sight of her in the Métro. We all stood cheek by jowl in an appalling intimacy, but she's a small woman. She insinuated herself unobtrusively into gaps, she kept her book level and she went on reading all the way. She didn't loiter as she paced across the city, but I kept her in sight down the back streets, not twenty metres behind her as she clicked briskly along the *quais* and over the bridge. She never hesitated and she never looked back. She stepped over the clear water rushing in the gutters with the elegance of a heron, she paused for a moment in the sunlight on the Pont St-Louis and I ducked behind a kiosk shaped like a giant orange. But she didn't turn round, just looked up, into the sun. And her dark hair swung gleaming with some new, strange, sinister, glossy sheen. To me she had become a stranger, all her gestures like secrets revealed. She marched down the rue St-Louis and turned into the hotel with a flick of her skirt, leaving me with the rest of the day to kill, watching the doors.

It wasn't one of the nights when she was on reception so she should have left at five. And so she did. Her sister came out and they stood chatting in the street for a moment before she turned away. I leant back behind a cinema poster as she would come my way towards the bridge. But she didn't. She walked the other way towards the Pont de Sully. I was waiting for this. But even so I felt sick in my stomach with anger and fright. She really was seeing another man. And I would soon know where he lived.

I started after her, ready to kill.

She never looked round. Not once. And she walked fast, with devastating precision. I tried to keep up with her as she forged her way on up the rue Cardinal Lemoine. She chose her route round the scaffolding with habitual certainty; she strode up the road without pausing for breath. She was fitter than I was, but I kept her in sight. When she got to the Place de la Contrescarpe I lost her. All of a sudden. There were plenty of people in the cafés, music from an organ-grinder positioned under the trees, the restaurants laying out for the evening: she must have entered one of the buildings. There were several huge siege doors with entry-phones. Not necessary, if she knew the code. I sat in one of the cafés, waiting. I stared at all the windows looking over the square, anxious and enraged. Was it there? Or there? Or behind those locked and dusty shutters? I was unable to touch the beer placed before me.

By ten o'clock I was desperate. Dusk had quietened the square. I could hear only their groans of satisfied desire and whispered love. People stared at me; a man who had once had a desirable wife. The man she had abandoned. Then I saw her, neat, calm, her shawl carefully arranged over her shoulders, stepping out of the great doors on the other side of the square. Her white face was luminous in the dusk. There was someone behind her. My heart shuddered to a halt as she turned to say goodbye.

He was tiny, almost a dwarf, bald, turning fifty, in a shabby brown suit. He was moon-faced, graceless, ugly. I did not attempt to hide. I sat there, staring. He took her hand, spoke to her for a moment – but I was too far away to catch their words – then he kissed her fingers reverently as if she was his patron saint. She bowed and turned away. She was gone, along the other side of the empty square, into the greying dusk.

I sat there alone, for a long, long time, staring at the grey outlines of the buildings, the grey trees drained of colour and the lights coming on in the upper windows. At last I drained the beer in one gulp. But I couldn't bring myself to move. I just sat there; all my jealousy and anger disintegrating into contempt.

Then, near eleven o'clock I got up and went home.

She was already in bed, the lamp casting shadows across her face. As usual, she was reading. I stood staring at her incredulously. For now I really was staring at a woman I had neither known nor understood, a monster who took her sexual pleasure in perverted ways, searching for freaks in sleazy back streets. She neither spoke nor looked up.

I told her that she was a whore. That I knew everything. That I had followed her. That I now understood her extraordinary behaviour. That I had seen her leaving him in the doorway. That it was useless to lie or to pretend any more. I found myself shouting.

She put down her book, marking her place with her glasses, pushed back the covers and got out of bed. Then she reached past me, so close I could have touched her, and turned on all the lights: the overhead lights, the wall lamps in the lounge, the halogen standing lamp next to the television. Stepping backwards, her face set with defiance, she swooped downwards with a gesture graceful as a ballerina and flung off her long cotton nightgown.

I reeled against the door.

Her body was utterly transformed. Striding her nipples was the handle of a dagger, its swirls curling her pink points, the blade severing her stomach in straight, firm, blue lines, riding the curves of her breasts. But from her pubic hair, rising sinister out of the dark, curly mass, coiling about the dagger's blade, was a deep red rose. In the full glare of the lights I saw every detail, her terrible clarity and aggression. On the dagger's hilt, unfurling like a medieval scroll, were the words *Death Before Dishonour*. Her tattoos shone menacing in the hard, white light.

Then she spoke.

"I have planned this for a long, long time. I have done it again and again in my dreams and now it is finished. Yes, sometimes it did make me ill. It was a long piece of work. But for me, the pain, even the infections, were important. It was my way of changing my body, irrevocably and for ever. You may think you changed me. But you didn't. I am like sand under your

feet. Each tide washes me clean. But I felt dishonoured every time you touched me. I shall never let you touch me again."

The River and the Red Spring Moon

We first noticed that something was wrong early in the morning on the way into town. There is a sharp corner by the farm on the hill with a dangerous hidden gateway, out of which come the tractors, usually backing up, plough first, the curved blades gleaming like spikes on a chariot. I had slowed right down to take the road descending towards the river when we saw the police cars, the ambulance, and the armed men with dogs. The invading presence was ranged along the damp banks. I crawled down the hill in first gear, staring.

The still green river, flanked by geometric lines of poplars, gave nothing away. There were no boats on the surface, no fishermen's umbrellas, curving alien shapes among the reeds. People gathered around their rusty cars on the bridge, watching patiently. It was raining, but nobody moved. They stood silent in the cold, still damp, watching. Along the bank, among the yellow wild irises and cow parsley prowled the gendarmes, prodding the grass. Two dogs sniffed purposefully at the edge, their tails raised like flags. The men in white leaned against the ambulance, smoking. There was no noise, no alarm, just the slight movements of the dogs searching the banks. I stopped the car for a moment and we too became part of the grey frieze of waiting figures. No one spoke to us.

We drove on into town, speculating. Was it an accident or a murder?

Later that night we heard that a prisoner had escaped. Had he swum the river and drowned? If so, he was less than one hundred metres away from the bridge. This hypothesis made no sense and was quickly discounted. Had he been hunted by the police and dogs right up to the river? There was a prison at Saintes. But the nearest institution which most closely resembled a prison was the madhouse in Angoulême. I locked up the doors of the barn and the outhouses, which I usually left open at night.

On the following day the rain fell heavily: slabs of heavy, grey spring rain pounding the geraniums. I relit the fire and spent the morning chopping wood. The temperature dropped. The remaining tulips sagged and splayed open, disintegrating in the mud. We cooked a huge stew and turned on the television. There was nothing about the escaped prisoner on the local news.

The rain had eased to a constant drizzle by the next day, but it was still uncomfortably cold in the morning. We drove into town, eager and curious to see what had happened on the bridge. The glassy green surface of the river lay before us, speckled with drops. There were still cars haunting the banks; rusty, ancient 2CVs and a Renault 21, the boot tied up with frayed string. Old men in old coats stood aimlessly in groups all along the banks. I stopped the car and went up to a woman who was waiting. She leant against the side of a decaying truck, her hair shining slightly with raindrops. We looked at each other for a moment or two. She still wore her apron and clogs, as if she had interrupted her work for a while to come down to the bridge.

"What's happened?" I asked.

"Someone has disappeared," she said.

I nodded and stood beside her in the rain.

"We saw the emergency services," I said. "Yesterday."

"They couldn't find him," she said, her voice neutral.

I didn't ask who he was. Or if she knew him. Or if he really was an escaped prisoner. I simply stood beside her in the rain, gazing at the river. Then I shook hands quickly, got back into the car and drove on. My hand tingled, as if I had been stung by nettles.

A week later I took the car in for a service. Monsieur Rousseau asked me if there was anything special that needed to be repaired. I didn't think so. I said that there was no hurry and that he could keep the car all day. He drove me back to the farm and as we approached the bridge I told him about what we had seen. Two cars were still there, waiting.

"Ah, you don't know the story?" he said. "The man who has disappeared used to live on the hill. He was her second husband. Years ago, his brother – it was his brother who was first married to her – drowned in the river. No one knows whether it was an accident or suicide. Same family. Then the widow remarried. She married the younger brother. And now he's gone. They won't find him now. Not until the river rises again. He's probably caught in the reeds at the bottom. The river is very deep, you know, towards the mill. There, it's bottomless. November maybe, they'll find him. The family is from around here. There were fifteen of them, brothers and sisters."

"How old was he?" I asked.

"Fifty-ish. The dogs found his tracks, leading to the edge of the river."

"Was it suicide?"

Monsieur Rousseau took his hands off the wheel and waved them about.

"*Alors, là . . . on ne sait pas.*"

I begin to exchange clichés with the neighbours. "*La pauvre . . . deux fois dans une vie . . . mais vous savez, une famille comme ça . . . c'est quand même bizarre . . . oui, deux frères . . . avec des histoires d'accidents, on sait jamais . . .*" There are no certainties.

It was the time of the red spring moon. The weather remained stormy, rainy, disturbed. We waited for the *saints de glace* to pass. No change was expected before the fourteenth of May. Day after day the chickens pecked in the thick wet grass, retreating to the barn as the rain came down. And every day there were cars still waiting on the bridge. A knot of pilgrims hovering in the dusk, gazing at the green stillness. I nodded to the waiting spectators, but no longer stopped to ask for news. The river yielded nothing.

Then one evening, when the fire was lit and the cats were sleeping peacefully among the cushions, I went out.

It has been raining all day. At eight o'clock the light still hangs in the sky, the water shines on the roadway. I risk going round to the neighbours in boots and hat to ask them if they will feed my cats and chickens while I am in Paris. As I walk back down the road the swifts suddenly surround me in the dusk, looming out of the grey damp, swooping close to the road, rising, curving like fighters against the wall, passing so close that it seems extraordinary I cannot catch them. I stand watching their performance: a troop of acrobats on an invisible trapeze. They rise, arch, dive, rushing against the shutters, balking at the iron gateway, their split tails elegant as evening dress. I become just one more of the obstacles which form the limits of their stage. They pass closer, hurtling straight towards me in a suicidal trajectory, then rising, banking, diving away in the final second before the inevitable collision. Their wing-tips skim the puddles and the curled leaves of the frost-blighted geraniums. The rain begins again and the swifts steady and gather, slowing their extraordinary dance. Suddenly I sense their collective cunning, their intelligence, and I retreat into the gateway, my cheeks burning as if I have been stung. The last one, white front, white mask, hiding the steadiness of his glare, swoops almost against me, pushing me out, forcing me into the courtyard. The sky darkens into twilight. I go inside and shut up all the doors.

At night, sometimes in the squally gusts of cold rain, sometimes shadowed by the red spring moon, a woman walks along the banks of the river, stepping carefully through the damp grass close to the current. Miles away, I can hear her. But she is not crying. She is singing.

James Miranda Barry
1795–1865

The moths plunge towards the lamp. I sit here at my desk, smoking to keep off the mosquitoes, listening to the sharp, brilliant sounds of the tropics, the roar of the night, frogs, crickets, weird cries in the bush, the dogs howling against their chains. The hospital reports are neatly stacked, separate from the accounts. I look with satisfaction upon my own unblotted, immaculate hand. I have a new steel pen. And I shall scratch my way across the official paper, sheet after sheet after sheet, perfected for the archives, posterity, history. I have always gone in for all the latest inventions. If it works, I will make use of it. Other men fear innovation, change crumbling their easy lives. I never have.

I lean back, breathless with heat, my tongue on fire from the chillis in my supper. I have a native cook. And we eat the same food. Sometimes served in a calabash. If we have no company I eat with my hands. Does that shock you? I am not surprised. So many of the other officers pretend that they are still in England and import their own men. They keep a fine wire netting between themselves and this humid island. Drenched in sweat, they struggle in stiff collars, evening dress, pickle their nights in alcohol, die young from yellow fever. White men will never do well here. They count the months of their postings, hide in the mountains all summer long, buy black women from the village men. If any man on my staff dares to touch my women who work in the hospital, he is sacked. I see to that personally. I investigate every complaint. And I believe what the women say. I have absolute standards.

Listen to the buzz of insects against the screen. My tobacco smoke hangs blue in the shadows. I watch a small patrol of cockroaches moving off the edge of the carpet. Beautiful things, hard black shapes, a marching mass of claws. This night, despite the smell, which is very disagreeable, I have not the heart to kill them. I am not always sentimental. We found a colony in the rotten wood beneath the verandah a week ago. I ordered them to be burned.

I have watched death daily here, in the hospitals, among the shacks in the villages, in the cool, polished white houses on the great estates. The smell of death never leaves my nostrils. I drench my uniform daily with rose water. The flowers mock my profession, hibiscus, bougainvillaea in torrents against the hospital steps, orange, white, pink sweet frangipani, daily at odds with putrefying flesh, pus oozing from raw sores, the smell of fresh blood. I travel a good deal, of course. An epidemic of one sort or another among the regiments can always be counted upon. Nights like this, peaceful, solitary; they seldom come to me.

I glance at the newspapers. We get them months late. Society events long past, scandals already forgotten, illnesses which have since done for the sufferer. Tonight I will not waste my solitude with stale news. Instead, I set aside the last reports and lower the wick on the lamp. Shadows lurch across the room. My servant appears at once in the doorway. He waits, waits, waits every night for his master.

"No, lad, go to bed now. Call me at the usual time in the morning. I will lock up the doors and fetch my own water. Leave me now. Goodnight."

Loosen my cravat, cuffs, braces, remove my top studs. Light another cheroot. Tonight it will be my turn to watch. To remember. And now the shrieking night bides the hours with me.

I dream the frost. Frost sealed the studio windows; the bare panes, luminous and opaque passed on the cold into the huge, cobwebbed vault, into the wooden joists, leaping up into the dark. The iron stove, humming peacefully, made very little difference to the air outside its immediate reach. The dark rafters hung with cold, and the great canvases, leaning against the bare walls, stuck together by the creeping frost. The water had frozen over in the bucket by the empty copper. A man, shrunken inside a greatcoat, moved like a fly before a huge, unfinished painting dealing with an historical subject. The figures moving in the paint might have been Romans, their swords and cloaks flickered red in the shifting light of the tallow candles. A horse's nostril flared, then vanished. There was one candle stuck to the rim of the cracked slab of glass he was using as a palette. His hands, encased in fingerless mittens, occasionally hovered above it. The firelight was just visible through the grid at the bottom of the stove, making great shadows dance at the man's feet. He moved slowly, a lumbering distorted monster. Soft creaks, gentle scratchings and the odd, choked thud of the falling logs were the only sounds rimmed by frost. Then the door opened, disturbing the cold air and a small child stood at the top of a dark flight of stairs.

She had risen in the dark and now she paused like an apparition, the unsummoned ghost. The man stared for a second, then ignored her. Without turning round he said, "Shut the door. There's a wind coming up the back staircase."

"Won't make any difference here." Her voice was like that of an adult. Suddenly, she took on the unexpected aspect of a dwarf.

"I said shut the door," the man repeated tonelessly and went on working. She shut the door with unnecessary force and the frost shimmered on the inner panes with the vibrations. Then the silence closed round the two figures, one hardly moving before the still painting, the other silent on a dusty stool by the stove. The frost grew, stealthily, from the guttering, coating the roofs white in the darkness.

For a long time the child stared at the picture, mumbling the edge of the dress in her mouth. She stared and stared, until at last she saw the huge, fleshy thighs of the Sabine women looming out of the candlelight. Suddenly her high dwarf's voice rose in the frost. "I shall never marry," she said.

The painter ignored her completely, so she said it again.

This time he spoke to me, without turning round, working steadily at the red muscles of a ravishing Roman arm. "Then, child, you must become a man. Learn to live in this world. Earn your own money. And stay out of debt."

He laughed bitterly at the painting. He said nothing more. He went on working.

I have spent my life in exile, ferociously guarding my privacy, travelling the world, searching out hot climates, courting danger, discovery, court-martial, disease. I have never been wealthy. I have never been loved. On my desk I have a small old-fashioned miniature, a silhouette of a woman with her hair piled in curls. If anyone is so imprudent as to inquire after the original I tell them that it is my mother, in tones which indicate I will not welcome further inquiry. Often the questioner apologizes, or murmurs their deepest sympathy. But this woman is not my mother. I met her years ago, in some lost corner of the colonies. She was beautiful, angry and bored. I was a junior officer, reticent, morose and hard-drinking. She asked me to dance, assuring me that in the wilderness where we found ourselves this was quite the done thing.

I corrected her upon this point. What she pleased to term a wilderness in fact possessed an indigenous culture of a nature so sophisticated that it in many ways surpassed our own. She bowed in acknowledgement as we took the floor and said, quite seriously, "I see that we are both radical in our opinions. We shall get on very well together."

And she looked straight into my face, unblushing, like a
street girl. "And am I also to assume, sir, that we are in all
respects alike? Small, red-haired and bad-tempered?"

"Your stature and colouring, madam, only add to your
charm. Your temper remains to be revealed."

"Thank you for the compliment. It is only fair of me to
inform you that your temper has a grand reputation and has
preceded your arrival. Is it true that you fought a dozen duels
in Africa and killed your man every time?"

This was not a promising beginning to our acquaintance.
But it did not end there. She wrote to me, visited me once
at the hospital during my rounds. I sent her packing, of course.
She was like a fly in hot weather. I could not be rid of her.

After six months I relented. Her parents were away. She
was alone with her sixteen-year-old brother and the servants.
I joined them for dinner, in full regimentals. There were no
other guests. The boy and I drank liquor at the table until he
was almost unconscious with the heat. We laid him out like
a gentleman. Then she raised her eyebrows at me, still
unblushing. Yes, this was the woman who, after I had
pleasured her so many times that the sheets were wet with
her happiness, reached for the studs on my shirt. I held her
at arm's length, away from my body, smiling in the candlelight.
I felt her tense and uncomprehending – then came the
moment of exhilaration, recognition, joy. Holding the candle
to my face, her eyes gleamed like fireflies in wet guinea grass.

"What are you?" she said.

"You know," I replied. And I covered her damp breasts in
kisses, all of which she repaid in full.

There was talk, of course. I really did fight a duel on her
behalf, killed the man and was posted elsewhere as a result.

Water. All the water I touch is polluted. My servants even
boil the water they bring to me every morning. I see water
muddied with antiseptic. Swabs awash with germs and disease,
dressings piled in the iron buckets for burning. The only water

I can endure, clean, sharp, the salt wind rising, is the sea. I spend this night walking the beach. The coconut palms lean out in the darkness, sand blown against the roots. I feel the breath of the undertaker's wind upon my cheek, the slow lift, slap and gurgle of the retreating tide. My boots' imprint vanishes at once in the soft sand. The earth renews itself. We leave no trace.

Then I see them, sitting in a circle. Big black women from the village, squatting like gods, smoking in darkness, or chewing the leaf. They are talking. They ignore my approach. One woman, her headscarf superb as an Egyptian crown, leans slightly towards me. "Evenin', Doctor."

I bow to the group. I do not speak.

"Is all right, man. Siddown." Her teeth flashed in the dark. "Siddown. We know what y'are."

Damp sand clings to my buckles, to my face, to the roots of the coconut palms. We watch the surf break, glimmer and vanish. The women continue to speak – in a language I do not understand.

I sit among them, contented. Here, at last, I am no longer misunderstood.

The Woman Alone

I am the woman alone. The woman who courts the shadows.
The woman who seeks – the darker side of the streets. The
woman armed. The woman who waits.

In the early days I used to go to rock concerts. I inhabited
vast halls or dark clubs, acres of barren grass where far in the
distance a group of shaggy men hammered away at their
guitars. I leant against a horse chestnut in the gardens, a joint
between my lips, my bare breasts encircled by painted daisies.
I made love with men who dressed up in flowered silks or the
skins of Tibetan yaks. Cheap joss sticks burned in the dark.
I painted my eyelids purple and wore overwhelming perfumes. I lived in rooms with black ceilings and dark green
walls. The rent was low in the centre of the city. I made the
lampshades myself, stitched beads to the rim. I took drugs in
the night and watched illusions illuminate the world.

I was easy on the eye and easy in the bed, a cooperative
sort of woman, who took the pill religiously, stayed skinny on
the dope and never made scenes.

I joined a Marxist reading group to amass information. I
became the woman of a man well known for his incisive grasp
of dialectic, his knowledge of Hegel (in German), his arrogant
superciliousness and his visit to Cuba. He was the leader of
our cell. We elected him because he would not tolerate dissent.
He never noticed my silences, but the group became afraid of
me. I would sit smoking, masked by dark glasses, cryptic and
intimidating. Nobody knew what I thought. I am the woman

who never speaks. I sit in seminars, lecture halls, political meetings, encounter groups. I am the woman who never speaks. My silence is never consent.

I became bored with Hegelian dialectics. I lived alone and worked in offices. I wore tight short skirts and read long books. I polished my nails and decorated my face. I slept with men who wore suits and ties and worked in other offices. Sometimes they raved about houses with lawns, children in pushchairs and holidays in *gîtes*. Sometimes they became importunate. I immediately cast them off. I am the woman who makes no demands. But I make no commitments.

One evening I went to a women's group meeting that was advertised in a magazine. I was dressed no differently from the other women there. I had been careful to remove my nail polish and lipstick, to suppress all but one earring and to sulk glumly in a corner under layers of drab clothes. At first no one spoke until a woman with huge sagging breasts talked about our freedom. I have desired nobody's freedom but my own. These women were not scientific. I was their visiting spy.

I listened. I signed their petitions, each time using a different name, ate their appalling nut cutlets, which ensured the freedom of beef, then slipped away into darkness. And the years passed.

I was tired of eating supper out of the saucepan, watching the television alone late at night, spending Saturday afternoons at the launderette, earning little money doing boring jobs, having nothing to say to other women when they talked about men. I was tired of being a woman alone. So I decided to marry a man in a suit and a tie.

The man I selected was very interested in sex. He had a university education. He liked to think about sex, talk about sex, watch women having sex, both with men and with other women in peculiar gymnastic positions, and then he liked doing it himself – a little. He had a good job marketing technical instruments. This may have given him ideas. He thought I was charming and had lived a radical lifestyle. He asked me about group sex in the Marxist cell. I invented salacious scenes spiced with Althusserian theories of sexuality and production. He asked about lesbianism in the women's groups. I told him that we masturbated together wearing high heels because this was the basis of feminist theory – that we should love our own bodies and have no inhibitions. He was thrilled by my stories and proclaimed me an intellectual of amazing powers. Unbelievable that I was still only a secretary. He would soon change all that.

My aunt came to the wedding. She wore a blue suit and sniffed. She told my husband how thankful my mother would have been that he wasn't the Marxist. His parents thought I was unsuitable because I was older than their beloved son. They were not well pleased. But they bore up well with their quiet, patient faces, the patient calm of the middle classes. We rented a large flat with hessian peeling from the walls. And they thought that was unsuitable too.

I gave up working and spent his money in shops. My part in this bargain was to listen and cook. I did both for three years. He became the sales manager. I got bored with the shops. He wanted a baby. I said I would think about it. For some reason he began smashing the furniture and weeping. Then he threw my contraceptives down the lavatory. I asked him the meaning of this puzzling behaviour. And he could give me no explanation.

So we purchased a house in the suburbs.

Our house was a new house on a new estate. We had an open-plan front lawn, shared with the neighbours, which we mowed alternate weekends in the growing season. We came to an amicable arrangement over the vista of green. But we had our own lawnmower and so did the neighbours, kept at the back, in separate sheds. No, the lawnmower was never shared. Nor were the back gardens; two wooden barriers, sodden with creosote stretched away for fifty yards, laden with trellises and flanked by roses, bordered with perennials. My husband dealt with the garden.

I began to hate all growing things. I surreptitiously swallowed the necessary chemicals and did not become pregnant. He groaned and thrashed and hoped upon my body in the dark. I destroyed his efforts at every turn. After six months of disappointment he became suspicious. And hunted about in the kitchen cabinets. It was time to go.

I spent hours at the garden centre, purchasing enough poison to kill the entire garden in three days. It is no small task, to poison the earth. I cooked him one last wonderful meal, his favourite beef casserole, seasoned with garlic and ginger, the onions finely chopped. I gave him a lot to drink.

I am the woman who moves in the night, the woman who changes her name, the woman who swims with a mighty arm, who surfaces somewhere else. I am the woman alone.

From then on I became anonymous. I was a secretary, a receptionist. I like clean jobs, front jobs, jobs where you have to dress for the part. Once more I wore the lipstick, repolished my nails, put on the paint, the varnish, the short skirts, the high heels, my wedding ring. I worked in a large publishing house, pressing the buttons on the switchboard, saying, "His number's ringing for you", "Would you like to speak to his secretary?", "I'm afraid he's away this week", "Do you have an appointment?" I became excellent at delivering these phrases so that they were charged with suspense, with possibility.

I began to make plans.

My silent helpfulness caught the eye of one of our junior trade representatives. He was a handsome young man who liked women that smiled and listened. He asked me out for a drink. When he came downstairs, a little late, I had already subdued the photocopier, locked up the files and tidied both my office and the reception desk. I had turned on the Ansaphone and checked the wastepaper basket in case anything important had been thrown away. I was sitting demure and upright with my knees clenched together on a hard chair by the door. My performance was perfect. He began to apologize for making me wait. I murmured not at all, not at all.

I am the woman who waits. We went to a complacent pub and he chose a corner of the saloon bar with cushions covered in roses. I drank one gin and tonic with ice and lemon. He drank a pint of Guinness. He talked about himself. I listened, smiling. The sweat trickled down my back. I am the woman who never speaks. My silence is never consent. He offered to walk me home. I insisted, quietly, but firmly, on taking a bus. He was a gentleman and did not persist.

He asked me out to dinner ten days later.

We went to an Italian restaurant and I ordered cannelloni so that I did not look ridiculous sucking spaghetti. He talked about his ambitions and his parents. I listened and smiled. He drank more of the bottle than I did and when I attempted to pay half the bill his hand covered mine as I clutched my cheque book. He took my arm as we approached his car. And I did not resist. I had laid my plans carefully. This was all foreseen. We sat in the front of a dark blue Ford Cortina looking through the windscreen at the fading light. Neither of us would begin.

"Would you like to come home with me?" he asked simply.

I am a woman who likes simple gestures. I nodded my assent. His apartment was comfortable, untidy. A pile of damp clothes was still loitering in the washing machine. His shelves were filled with difficult books by South American writers and contemporary philosophers. His desk was covered with papers. His bed was unmade, the duvet coiled into dramatic, volcanic shapes. But the washing up was clean and dry on the draining board.

I sat down on the sofa with my knees clenched tightly together, my skirt stretched carefully across them. He offered me coffee. I asked for more wine. Delighted, he went away to the basement and returned with an excellent bottle of Burgundy, covered in British dust. I stared into the wine.

I am the woman alone. The woman who looks out into

great distances. As I stared into the red darkness I saw my own silent, smiling face, like Christ's image in the sweatcloth of Santa Veronica, rising to meet me. I looked up. The young man was standing over me, intent on the first kiss of the night, which would constitute our bargain sealed. I drank the wine and stood up.

I am the woman alone. The woman whose body is staked to the screen, to the boards, to the page. I am the woman you dream. I am the woman who walks in the night. I am the woman who seeks – the darker side of the streets. I am the woman who ups the price. I am the woman who opens her legs. I am the woman who never makes scenes. I am the place where you drown.

He did not speak to me for over a week. He did not dare. I was not exactly what he had expected. I had been so silent and so helpful. I had listened so quietly. I had taken notes. He never came down to my office. He never rang up. I sharpened the tips of my nails with an iron file – and waited. Then I met him by chance in the town. He was staring into the window of a hairdresser's. He had lost weight. His cheeks were already yellow and terrible. The night of his perishing had already begun. I steadied the strap of my handbag on my shoulder and stood beside him. He gazed at me, appalled. But his desire overpowered him.

"May I visit you this weekend?" he asked, with bizarre politeness.

"It is unlikely that you could ever find where I live. I do not live in this city."

He stared at me as if I had gone mad. I bent down and picked up a round cobblestone that was loose beneath my feet.

"Look," I said and flung the stone down the pavement low to the ground, skimming the ruts, ricocheting off the wheel of a pushchair, the hubcap of a car, the rim of a bicycle wheel. When he turned again, an exclamation on his lips, I was gone.

I am the woman whom men demand. I am the woman who is wonderfully well paid. I am the woman who moves in the night, who drives her own cars, who pays in cash. I am available for work, for hire, for the fulfilment of your every desire. Call me on Freephone 0800 382 683. Toll free from the States, all contracts undertaken. Half payment in advance, the rest on delivery. I am the woman who sets the terms. I use no weapons but the ones I was born with. My scope seems enlarged with the years. I speak many languages, take many shapes. I am the woman you cannot remember, the woman you never forget. I am the woman who does your will. I am the woman who kills.

The Crew from M6

I remember the house. You can't see it from the road and we almost missed the turning, which was hidden by dusty white bushes. The gate was rotten and decrepit, hanging inwards from the stakes over the ditch. The drive curved upwards, steep, uneven, pitted gravel, clearly a murky river after the thunderstorms. We looked up into the bush, oak trees, thorns and broom, long past flowering, the brown pods already formed, but we couldn't see the house. At no point on the drive can you see the house. It was very early in the morning, just gone eight o'clock, but the dew was already vanishing as the thermometer climbed. We had bottles of Badoit in an ice box, all the equipment stored in the boot, the monitor and some of the lighting controls packed in with Sébastien on the back seat. Everything lurched backwards as we pulled up the hill. It's a powerful car, but we had to go up in first gear.

Even when you entered the clearing it was hard to gauge the size of the house. We saw a mass of worn red brick and white stone, with white stone steps leading down on to the grass, geraniums in pots, recently watered while they were still in shadow, the shutters open all down one side of the house, but on the other side only slightly ajar, letting cracks of white light into the darkened rooms. There was no one in the courtyard. No one came out to meet us. Jean-Michel got out and shouted, "Anybody home?" And the house stared silently back. I had the feeling that we were being watched. We all got out of the car and Jean-Michel climbed the steep stone steps. It was too dark to see properly inside, but peering up I had the impression of polished wooden floor-boards, a mirror over a carved sideboard with wooden vines wound around columns on the corners, and a German helmet from the Great War poised above a gun, mounted on the other side of the passage so that they were reflected in the mirror. Jean-Michel knocked on the doorframe and called inside, "Anybody home?" There was no answer.

He stood on the top of the steps, a circle of sweat already showing under his arms, looking around. "You haven't made a mistake, have you, Isabelle? It was today that they were expecting us?" he shouted down to me.

"Yes, today. I'm quite sure. I spoke to one of them the day before yesterday. I said eight o'clock so that we would be able to film during the day."

"Then where are they?"

He made an impatient gesture. Sébastien opened a bottle of Badoit and leaned against the car door, drinking directly out of the bottle. Jean-Michel came down the steps and set off round the house in search of our subjects. I heard a dramatic cackle of chickens as he turned the corner and vanished. I looked carefully at the water still settling on the geraniums. There were still drops on the leaves, perfect shining circles of pure water. The geraniums, pungent and acid in the sun, had only just been watered. Someone had been here only moments before. Again, I had the feeling that I was being watched. Someone was waiting, waiting to see what I would do. Waiting.

Badoit in hand, Sébastien wandered off in search of the view. The oak woods pressed around the house, but occasionally, through the green, I could see the blue shape of wooded hills and white rocks. There were no other houses nearby. I put on my hat and sat down on the steps with my back to the house. It was eight-thirty. And I'm sure it was eight-thirty, because I looked at my watch. Then someone touched my shoulder. I started up.

She was standing on the step behind me, smiling; a tall, thin woman with dark hair cut very short. She spoke French with a strong English accent.

"Have you been waiting long? I am so sorry. I'll call the others." She had a very sharp face, a sallow, leathery skin, as if she had spent too many summers in the sun. I couldn't have guessed her age correctly within ten years.

"Oh, I'm sorry," I began, "I didn't hear you." She simply smiled and turned away. A moment later the steps were empty again. It was very disconcerting. I was irritated. Then I heard voices from behind the house and there was Jean-Michel, triumphant, with three women pattering beside him, all talking at once.

"*Bonjour . . .*"

"*Désolée . . .*"

"We were feeding the animals . . ."

They talked in chorus.

"This is Patricia. Who owns this house. *Notre Anglaise.* I am Brigitte. We spoke on the phone. This is my friend Sylviane." We were all shaking hands and gabbling nervously at each other. I looked hard at the Englishwoman. She was about thirty-five or forty, large, red-cheeked and very friendly. She welcomed us into her house. She was not the same woman I had seen on the steps.

"I'm so sorry that we made you wait," said Patricia. The accent was the same, but the voice was quite different. I shouted to Sébastien from the top of the steps.

"Sébastien! *Viens!*"

And I looked at my watch. It was then that the uncanny sensation returned. It was eight-twenty. I must have been mistaken. And yet I am sure that I had not been mistaken. Sébastien pushed his way out of the bushes, green plastic bottle in hand. We had another round of nervous introductions. And then, one after another, we all entered the house.

The women all talked at once. Brigitte was the most striking: a woman in her middle years, her age unguessable, hair cut short like a page boy, sharp brown eyes and a lined square face. She had a frankness and sensuality in her gaze, an openness that was startling, unguarded. I liked her at once. Sylviane smoked continuously. She had a sharper, more pointed face, a strong Midi accent, and was more obviously nervous. I noticed that the Englishwoman had bitten fingernails. She wore no rings. The woman I had seen on the steps did not appear again.

We sat in the kitchen, which was cool and dark. Baskets hung from the ceiling and the old floor tiles were damp and clean, water still present in the cracks. A huge fireplace took up one wall; there was a barbecue grill with charred brass knobs propped against the internal wall beside the great blackened fire irons. I noticed that there were still scraps of fat clinging to the grill. The room smelt of woodsmoke and coffee. An enormous engraving hung over the mantelpiece with bunches of dried lavender attached to the corners. I tried to work out the meaning of the image which appeared to represent the apocalypse. There were anguished crowds pushing against one another and strange square buildings illuminated by lightning in the background. But it was too dark to see clearly. Where the sun crashed through the shutters, glamorous shafts of light fell upon ordinary things, a coffee percolator, a bowl of rotting peaches, a polished silver fork, plates stacked on a dresser. Brigitte and Jean-Michel were dominating the discussion.

"You have to understand why we mistrust you people like the plague," said Brigitte, but without aggression. "We are so tired of being misrepresented in the media. The public think that we are some kind of erotic thrill. That we don't have lives other than sexual lives."

"But that's why we are making this film," Jean-Michel declared, "we want to show you as you really are. The idea was to meet you on holiday – relaxed and at home – as you are now. And then, after *la rentrée*, to film you at work, following your daily lives . . . to show how you do resemble everyone else."

The Englishwoman interrupted. "Why do you want to eradicate our difference?" she asked sharply. She had made us all coffee and had said nothing so far. "I am not like you and have no wish to be so."

I suppose she must have realized how hostile this sounded as she went on to say, raising her bowl in a toast, "And I'm sure I drink coffee quite differently."

We all laughed nervously. But the discussion became franker, more relaxed, as soon as the lines of opposition were clearer. They were sceptics, disbelievers. I found their talk very disconcerting. They criticized everything: the media, the family, society, masculinity, sex. They seemed to think that all women were potentially discontented. None of them had ever wanted children and they all hated religion. They said that they knew women who had had children on their own by artificial insemination. I found this quite horrible, but Jean-Michel was desperate to be introduced to a woman who had done it and would take part in the film. I asked about their relations with their families and they all seemed to have close friendships with their mothers. But the Englishwoman, sensing my line of questioning, pointed out that she had been Daddy's girl, so that if I was looking for psychoanalytical explanations she would be only too happy to refute all my suppositions. They argued against us, firmly, politely, but uncompromisingly, blocking our proposals at every turn. I said that it must be very difficult to see the world so differently, and yet to live within it – on such different terms. All three of them agreed.

By ten o'clock the heat was stifling. Outside on the steps the glare clamped like a mask over our faces. Jean-Michel decided to begin filming the interviews outside, under the trees. He went off with the Englishwoman in search of a suitable spot. He wanted somewhere charming, the rural picturesque. I sat with Brigitte and Sylviane on the steps. They were at once more relaxed when the men vanished into the bushes, following the Englishwoman. I defended Jean-Michel.

"You mustn't think he's just a macho bully," I said, "he's very sincere about making this programme. After all, it's a controversial subject. He's prepared to risk his reputation. I know he sometimes seems overbearing. It's just his manner. He genuinely wants to understand you, to represent your point of view . . ."

The women nodded sympathetically and pityingly. I was very irritated. "You're very hard to know. Very hidden. It was almost impossible to find any woman who would speak to the camera. Jean-Michel wouldn't let anybody speak from behind a mask. He said it would run counter to the whole philosophy of the programme."

"And you? What do you think?" Brigitte demanded. "Tell us what you think."

"Me? Oh, I do the research. I had to find the subjects. It's not easy. I read all the specialist press. The men were easier. They're more public anyway. We have friends at M6 and in the other production companies, who introduced us to their friends. We've already got quite a few hours of tape. Some of which will be excellent. But finding the women . . . There were some who wouldn't agree to be filmed unless they had complete control of the final version. One of them brought her lawyer to the first interview. Can you imagine? There he was, sitting beside me, taking notes. I was very uncomfortable. I can't work like that. There has to be some sort of trust between the filmmakers and their subjects."

"But can't you see why there isn't?" demanded Sylviane.

"We're clear about our intentions. We want to present positive images."

"Yes. Of the zoo." The Englishwoman was standing at the bottom of the steps. She had left Jean-Michel raving over the picturesque beauty of an abandoned chicken coop which was to be immortalized in our film.

"You see," Patricia continued in her rapid, inaccurate French, "you've come out armed with all your liberal prejudices, which you don't know you have, to observe us in our natural habitat. Like animals. You get to interpret us *pour le grand public français*. All of whom are assumed to be like you. We are not holding the cameras. Therefore it is not our version."

I shrugged. They weren't exactly hostile. But there was no pleasing them.

"You say that the men are more public anyway," Brigitte continued. "Don't you ask yourself why? Why can they express their sexuality and live their lives more openly than we do? Have you asked yourself those questions?"

"We are more at risk," said Sylviane grimly. "I hope that you're not going to identify this house too closely. Or Patricia will find her sunflowers in flames, her chickens strangled on the doorstep and her cats full of bullets."

I looked up, shocked.

"I thought you had good relations with your neighbours."

"Nobody respectable likes living next to perverts," said Patricia sweetly.

"They've all got AIDS."

"They rape children."

" . . . and strangle grandmothers."

"They're a threat to the family."

"And the State."

"They're witches."

"Whores!"

"Schoolteachers."

"Alcoholics."

"Drug addicts."

"Thieves."

"They steal your husband."

" . . . and your wife."

"Shoplifters."

"Monsters."

"Perverts."

"Dykes."

Their chorus ended in the wicked, wicked laughter of complicity.

"So you see," continued Patricia, "there's a price to be paid for refusing to collaborate."

"Ahh," said Brigitte, stretching her bare toes out into the sunlight, "we haven't talked about *les collabos*."

This time I was really angry, because I was certain that they were getting at me. In any case, it is a shocking thing to accuse a woman of being a collaborator, as if men were enemies, an occupying power, an alien force.

"What do you mean?" I asked sharply, although I was perfectly aware of what they meant. Brigitte seemed to know this, for she swung round in the wind of my defensiveness.

"Do you live alone? Or with your bloke?" she asked directly.

"Alone. I have my own apartment."

"Could you live your life, do your work, earn your own money, be independent, as you are now – and live with a man?"

I hesitated.

"No. That's not yet possible. There would have to be compromises. On both sides. But I see what you're getting at. I know many women like myself and I think that men do find it hard to deal with independent women."

"*Voilà*," said Patricia cheerfully.

"I see," I said bitterly, "you don't think we should even try to change men."

"Why should they change something it's taken centuries to organize so nicely?" said Patricia scornfully. "Heterosexuality is a rather different deal if you're a man than if you're a woman."

She smiled at me with what I now realize was a character-istic mixture of acid and charm.

"If you're a man you get to have a hostess, a housekeeper, a mistress, a nanny and a cook. If you choose carefully you also get a wage-earning junior colleague. But if you're a woman you get to be a whore and a slave."

When someone has opinions like that there is no point in

talking about equality and partnership. They can't understand a word you say.

"This is the way we see things," said Brigitte, "there is a state of war, undeclared war, between women and men. For so long women have been slaves and men have been their masters. We are no man's slaves."

"Neither am I," I snapped.

"Bravo," said Sylviane, staring at me speculatively.

"How old are you?" asked Patricia.

"I'm twenty-nine."

"And do you want a house, a dog, two children and camping holidays abroad?"

She looked like a serpent when she said this.

"Well . . . I've always wanted children. And I wouldn't want them alone." I was thinking of their quite horrible descriptions of sperm in test tubes and gravy basters.

"Shortly then, you will have to choose," said Patricia.

"Between marriage . . ."

" . . . and independence."

"Freedom . . ."

" . . . and chains."

"I certainly don't intend to get married."

"Much wiser," said Brigitte, in pacifying tones. "One in three end in divorce."

"You're all very old-fashioned," I pointed out, "you've got pre-feminist attitudes. Men are much more modern now. They do their share of the work. You have an idea of heterosexuality that is very out-dated."

"Oooohh," shrieked Patricia, "my man is not like that. He believes in the equality of women. He's incapable of abuse, exploitation and oppression. He would never be aggressive."

"Never."

"Oh, never."

"And does he have you credited as his co-director? Does he acknowledge your work?"

The Englishwoman had a really evil expression. And suddenly I realized that she knew I was with Jean-Michel. How on earth did she know? They were very unkind. I was angry and hurt.

"Patricia. *Calme-toi*," said Brigitte.

"Listen," she turned to me, "other women are not our enemies. But there are women who support men's versions of femininity. Who endorse their power, mouth their words, curry their favour. And who deny us. We call these women the *collabos*. I know that some of them genuinely believe that their oppression is freely chosen. Some of them – probably quite sincerely – love every moment. But they degrade themselves. They had a choice as we did. Everyone has a choice."

"You're educated. You've all got jobs," I said. "How much choice does a poor Arab woman have?"

"Come down to our bar and ask them," snapped Sylviane. "Do you think I had a university education? When I was eighteen I was working in a factory. I've always worked in bars and restaurants. I'm not a university lecturer or a publisher. I was born in an HLM on the edge of Vence. Don't assume."

"I've found the perfect spot," cried Jean-Michel, bounding up the steps with the sweat pouring off him. "Do you have an extra long extension cable?"

And the discussion dispersed in the mid-morning heat.

Sylviane went back into the house to prepare an armada of cold drinks. The Englishwoman went in search of books and parasols to use as props. Brigitte walked beside me in the garden. Despite the heat, the garden seemed shady and cool. It was very overgrown and damp underfoot. In full sun behind us I saw a mass of arum lilies banked against the house, huge white trumpets raised to the sky. The wall of the house suddenly looked more massive, like a Cathar fortress: the body of the wall in narrow Roman brick, the facings around the windows in cracked white stone. The shutters were painted a strange, thick blue, with tiny lozenges in each one. Now they were almost shut against the savagery of the rising heat. We stood under the trees. I asked Brigitte why the wooded slopes and moss-covered steps were so damp, even in high summer. She told me that the hill had three springs, sacred to the Graces, and she laughed. The house was not linked up to the public water system, had its own septic tank and generated all the summer electricity from the solar panels on the barn. We walked carefully down the greening gravel path into the trees. I saw tiny blue and white flowers glimmering among the stones and ferns on the banks. I heard the trickle of falling water. We pushed our way through the damp foliage and then I could smell water and the musty freshness of wet earth.

There, just below us, was a tiny stone barricade with a clear green pool held back by a green bank coated in moss, lichens, and ferns spattered with green drops. The water poured gently out of the green rocks, as if the stones were alive and breathing. I took off my watch and plunged my arms into the water. Brigitte washed her face in the clear, cold spring, and smiled at me.

"Don't let the others bother you," she said. "They like you. That's why they're arguing. If Patricia likes someone a lot she gives them hell. To people she can't stand she is charming – then they fall out of her head as soon as she turns away. If she gets at you, it's because she thinks you're worthwhile."

"I'll try to remember that her bullying is a compliment," I said ruefully, "but who is the other woman? The one who is not taking part in the filming?"

"What other woman?"

"I saw her on the steps. Tall, thin, I think a bit older than you. Brown shirt, jeans – and a brown suede waistcoat. A bit old-fashioned. Very short hair."

Brigitte looked genuinely baffled. "*Mais, qui est cette femme?*"

I explained again what had happened, but I did not mention the peculiar slippage of time that I had noticed.

"It must have been one of the neighbours, leaving the milk or collecting eggs," said Brigitte, her face clearing.

"But she looked like one of you," I said, suddenly

embarrassed at naming the specificity of their difference. Brigitte noticed and laughed out loud.

"Ah, there you are. We could be any woman, you know. We are every woman."

She let the matter drop and so did I.

Jean-Michel had found the perfect spot; an abandoned chicken coop with a broken white door in warm brick under the trees, spattered with shadows and bright white light. All the wires and black boxes were being installed and connected. The ground sloped sharply. Sébastien was levelling the equipment with branches, sticks and bricks that had fallen out of the wall of the chicken coop. The camera lay like a dinosaur, inert in its case. The men then arranged the spotlights around a wrought-iron table on which Patricia had set up a pile of suitable books so that it would look as if Brigitte had been surprised, studying her own culture.

"I wouldn't like to do what you do," said Patricia, carefully placing paper and pencils in disarray, at Jean-Michel's commands. "You invent scenarios for documentaries in which everything is both superficial and fake."

"We make films that people can understand easily and enjoy watching," I said, nettled.

"Doesn't make it genuine."

"Nothing in the media is genuine. It has to be real life to be genuine."

"That's not a simple distinction," said Patricia thoughtfully, "real life is the life you value, the life you make real for yourself. Plenty of people have told me I don't live in the real world. But I do have a real life. It's the rest of the world that's got to change."

"Well, we won't do that with one television programme," I replied crisply.

Jean-Michel intervened with a very convincing burst of righteousness. "But if one person who sees this programme changes their mind about you I will have achieved what I set out to do."

Patricia raised her eyebrows speculatively. Brigitte trod on her foot. I saw her do it. And Patricia said nothing.

The filming began. We interviewed Brigitte on her own at the table, surrounded by the fake clutter of books and pencils. I sat just beside the camera with the sun corroding my left eye. Sébastien stood sweating with the boom suspended over his shoulders. He never said anything at all when we were filming and hardly ever spoke otherwise. To do him justice, so long as we were filming neither did Jean-Michel. I sorted my notes and chatted to Brigitte while they checked all the levels of light and sound. The landscape was not silent. We could hear the crickets and cicadas shrieking in the undergrowth, the constant trickle of water and the rustle of lizards in dry leaves. I felt my left elbow, caught in a block of sun, turning red. I asked Brigitte to remember her childhood, her father, her mother, her early life.

"That's only relevant if you're assuming that lesbianism is genetic, or has its origins in the Oedipal crisis," she said cheerfully, "I discovered my love for women through my political involvement with the women's movement."

This set the tone for the interview. She challenged the terms of my questions rather than answering them. All right, if that was how she was going to refuse the game. I laid down my carefully prepared notes, folded my arms and asked bluntly, "Why are you homosexual?"

"Why are you heterosexual?" she retaliated.

"Because it's natural." That let her tongue loose like a galloping horse.

"Natural? OK. So you get to say what is natural. Is it natural for men to abuse, rape and kill women? Is what's happening in Bosnia natural? Is war natural? A result of natural, healthy male aggression? Is capitalism natural? Is it natural for women to earn less than men? The very division between what is culturally determined or natural is a product of culture. You tell me what's natural and what isn't. People only defend something as natural when all other rational argument has failed. If something simply exists in nature, as women's love for women always ever has done, is it natural? You tell me."

This discussion should have shaken the camera. But Jean-Michel and Sébastien said nothing whatsoever; they went on filming. Brigitte elaborated her theory of sexual and political desire.

"One of Monique Wittig's slogans," she said, "is that '*Les lesbiennes ne sont pas des femmes*', and Patricia always says that doesn't quite work in English, because they can translate '*femmes*' with two words, 'women' and 'wives'. So that it can mean lesbians are not women – or not wives. But isn't it significant that our word for woman also means wife? I see why Wittig says that. We are not part of the economy of heterosexual desire, nor – or at least it's often the case – are we part of their economic and social structures either. We're certainly not part of their intellectual structures. I remember one married woman telling me that she found Wittig's work unreadable. Not because it was so especially difficult, but simply because Wittig's thinking was so alien. We are part of a search for other meanings of the word '*femme*'. I think that the liberty of lesbians is crucial for the freedom of women. We are the open door, the way out . . .

" . . . And desire between women? Well, it can be urgent, imperative, terrible – or it can be full of gentleness, tenderness. Lesbian desire doesn't operate on the heterosexual trajectory of the lover and the beloved. We are both lovers and beloved. Even in the universe of desire we are travellers, voyagers, explorers. There are no boundaries, no frontiers, no limits . . ."

"Well, that's all very idealistic," I interposed. "What are the limits you encounter in the everyday world?"

Brigitte smiled broadly, a shining gust of warmth and welcome. "You. And the poverty of the heterosexual imagination.

" . . . But of course," she went on, "women don't rule the world. Men do. The greatest obstacles to the realization of lesbian desire are men and masculinity."

The camera's red eye continued to watch her, unwavering. She proposed what sounded more like the abolition than the reconstruction of the gender system. I felt a headache approaching behind my left eye. I tried to shift the discussion away from a critique of the present sexual system and social arrangements towards the erotic and the personal. I had agreed with Jean-Michel that we should do.

"How do you make love with another woman?" I asked.

At last Brigitte lost her temper. Her eyes suddenly lightened and cleared. "I'm astonished that you – another woman – can ask me that question. Are you so fixated on masculine desire that you have no idea what kiss, what caress would give you pleasure? What do you like? Where do you like to be stroked and touched? Don't you know?"

There was a terrible dumbfounded silence. Then Brigitte said crisply, "Lesbian sexuality is women's sexuality. I'd have thought that was obvious."

I took a deep breath. Then I heard the snap of a branch breaking, the swift steps of someone passing over the leaves in the woods behind me. But no one else looked up. We were being watched. The sweat felt cold on the back of my neck. I made one last desperate attempt to control the interview.

"Tell us about your projects. About the Bar-Café and the *Café littéraire*."

Indeed, praxis turned out to be safer waters than theory. Brigitte narrated the history of their Bar-Café, the political importance of visibility in the public world and the emphasis on lesbian culture. She was lucid, practical, funny. The interview ended in laughter. It was nearly one o'clock. We were all covered in sweat.

"Good God," said Brigitte, "I've got two huge wet circles under my armpits. You aren't going to show that on M6, are you?"

"Oh no," said Jean-Michel, oozing solicitous good humour, "I enlarged the image so that we only see your face and shoulders. You look wonderful, with the light behind you on the chicken coop. *L'effet de contre-jour. C'est très beau.*"

We left them to cover up all the equipment in plastic and blankets and climbed back up to the house. Sylviane was waiting on the steps, now in shadow, smoking.

"Well, Isabelle," she smiled wickedly, "*pas trop traumatisée?*"

"I do find it disturbing," I said honestly, "in fact, very disturbing."

"Nobody likes being put in question," said Patricia. "Come and have a drink. You poor love, you must be fried to a crisp."

Lunch was laid out under the walnut trees at the back of the house. I sat drinking iced water, hearing the chickens clucking in the shadows, like the organ line in a fugue. Occasionally the cock shrieked from the stone guttering. All the food was cold and fresh, charcuterie with peppers laid like mines in the flesh, tomatoes, grated carrots spotted with mustard seeds, lettuce waiting to be turned in its dressing, pâté eyeing me from beneath a thin layer of fat, a crisp round hunk of bread, uncut beside the dark wine bottle which bore no label. There was nothing sinister or odd about the plastic tablecloth, the thick glass tumblers, and the chipped white plates. I felt anxious, dizzy and sick.

Patricia brought me two paracetamol tablets. "It's the heat," she said, "you're used to Paris. Drink lots of water. Here's a bottle of Badoit just for you. Take these for your headache."

We sat out in the shade, caught in the breath of warm air that slithered round the corner of the house. Looking up, I saw that there was another storey and an attic gable. The house was not symmetrical, which was unusual for this area, and yet it all appeared to have been built at the same time. I could not grasp its dimensions, which seemed to be in flux. Did that back staircase lead to the kitchen? The house sat with closed eyes, awake, crouched. The talk was general, easygoing. I noticed that the women were charming, chatty, inoffensive with the men. They sought out common areas of interest. They asked Jean-Michel about his award-winning documentaries. They listened while he boasted, handing him leading questions, to draw him out as women always do when they flatter men. I found their charm and warmth very pointed and disturbing. Their ease of manner, which seemed to have no undercurrents, suddenly appeared to me to be an impenetrable masquerade. Yet they were perfectly natural. They even drew Sébastien into the conversation. They discussed television, music, politics; at one point Patricia was championing the rights of minority language speakers and describing Druids in Wales. Jean-Michel turned to me and suggested that we should make a film about extant Druidic cults in Europe. I felt unease prickling my arms. I was utterly isolated. The men were alarmingly unobservant. They noticed nothing. They did not see that these women were linked by a thread, like birds in flight, wing-tips touching, knowing exactly when to bank, rise and swing out against the buffeting warm air. I perceived their rhythm, but could not enter their closed circle. I was like a child pressed to their glass, breathless and frightened.

Yet it was very difficult to say what was so frightening. They were so ordinary – and yet so ruthless. I thought, this is what it must be like eating with terrorists, utterly unremarkable people, who are capable of killing you.

By two-thirty the heat was dense and shimmering. We decided on a siesta under the trees and to begin filming again in the late afternoon. Patricia unfolded a wooden day bed and covered it in patchwork cushions. She licked her forefinger and raised it in the air, then placed the entire contraption in the only draught of cool wind that touched the wooded slope. I was being given the special treatment. Yet I could not sleep. The others dozed beside me. Sylviane and Brigitte talked for a while. The Englishwoman had vanished. I slept fitfully for an hour, then suddenly awoke, breathless and oppressed, the heat like a gag over my mouth. Everyone else was asleep.

I got up quietly and walked away into the woods.

The air was thick and still, the cicadas and crickets shrieking in the heat. The lizards rushed away from beneath my feet. I stumbled through patches of light and shade, the moss diminished and the ground became baked and hard. Cracks appeared in the earth. I followed a faint path through the foliage, sensing the crickets, ferocious as rattlesnakes, chattering in the baking green. I tried to take deep breaths, but the heat clamped across my chest like a furnace. I moved slowly, pushing against the barrier of burning air, leaning helplessly forwards, each step an effort. The colours around me were opaque, obscure. I could see two huge shadows of the chestnut trees below me, their green darkening, curling in the white light. I could smell mint, crushed under my feet; the shrill birds above, urgent, suddenly hushed. But the terrible impediment was the light, this thick, white, oppressive airless density. It was like pushing against a liquid, light transformed into liquid, a liquid burning, burning my face, my throat, my bare arms, shoulders at every step. I slumped down against the rough, chapped trunk of a chestnut tree.

I felt as if I had been drugged. Nothing was clear. There were no edges. One object became another as I stared, like an unfinished painting. I stared and stared at the huge spaces before me. Everything came too close to me and hovered, fluid, uncertain, illusory in the thick white light. I tried to breathe. I couldn't feel that I was breathing. I clutched the huge roots of the tree beside me and tried to make sense of the images translated by the heat. I saw the road below me. It was packed white dirt with a central brown line of dried grass. I was sure that it had been asphalted before, a small departmental, with the edges neatly mown. But now it was white earth, packed flat, well-used. And maize, I had remembered acres of maize, tall and dark green. I cannot have been mistaken. But here were sunflowers, yellow torrents of sunflowers, ripening now, huge, black cores expanding, the faded petals cast out to the rim, the black eyes like the sun's eclipse, magnified a thousand times in field after field after field. I put my hands up to my face. The sunflowers appeared unearthly, menacing in the white haze. As I watched, I saw each flower, the huge hot core packed with seeds, growing larger, darkening, great black single eyes ranked before me, knowing, darkening. Then there was nothing, no colour, no yellow, no green, just white, thick light and the huge dark cores, filled with seeds, magnifying the void.

I shut my eyes tight.

When I looked up again I was still sitting under the chestnut tree and the woman was sitting beside me, gazing out at the sunflowers. I peered at her carefully, her leathery hands and brown face, the skin pulled tight across the bones. She was so close to me that I could have touched her.

"Are you part of the household?" I asked.

She looked at me and smiled, the lines appearing like strange writing in her face.

"Have we met before?" I had the uncanny sensation that I had seen her somewhere else.

"Surely. Yes." She gazed at me calmly. The voice was clear and at ease, but came from a great distance.

"Where was that? I really can't remember."

There was something disquieting in her manner and her tone. I wanted to touch her.

"Follow me," she said, and got up. Then the heat hit me as if I had been slapped. Dazed, insecure, I put out my hands to her. She was still there, her outlines blurred, some distance off. One part of my mind stayed clear. I was convinced I was hallucinating. She could not be there. Yet a brown form moved down the rough path and stood, waiting patiently, on the road below. I felt as if my head was going to explode.

Standing on the roadway, the white earth burned my feet

through the soles of my shoes. I could not move or speak. All around me, at eye level, the sunflowers leered and stared. I had no sense of scale or time, simply the blur of slow asphyxiation. Then I saw, quite close, a large Renault Trafic van, surrounded by sunflowers. There were none broken or crushed in front of the van; it was encircled by perfect rows of sunflowers. I stared at this new apparition. It was in two colours, cream and dark red with a metallic sheen; the rear seats had been removed. As I stared at the van I saw the tassels forming a sombre chain round the windows. It was a hearse.

Then I became aware of a very small, earnest man standing beside me, anxious to shake my hand. The woman was there too, introducing him, as if it was very important we should know one another.

"This is Monsieur de Loom."

I became aware of her words rather than hearing them. Monsieur de Loom began to speak. I sensed that his long, explanatory discourse was urgent and consistent, but no single word made sense. He gestured, pointed, nodded, shrugged, and talked on and on. I stared at his face, his thin moustache, the kindly wrinkled folds of his cheeks, the lines circling his eyes, which deepened at each emphasis. I listened carefully and I understood nothing. Nothing. The woman smiled at me. As her face tightened I could see the skull beneath the skin.

I was suspended in an inferno, outside time, listening to a stream of words which had ceased, become crickets chafing the thick air. I saw things too close. A female praying mantis, huge, brilliant green, poised against the bark of the chestnut tree. She was too close, too close. I drew back, concentrating hard on putting one foot in front of another, up the slope, not looking to left or right, pushing back the boiling green. Pushing the branches away from my face, feeling my lips cracked beneath my tongue, feeling the sweat bubble in the crook of my arm. Don't look. Don't see. Don't listen to these eerie torrents of unintelligible explanation. They are sleeping. How can they lie sleeping, abandoned, vulnerable, displayed, not caring who is loose on their land? These women with the confidence of savages, who walk through one world while seeing another. I want to shake them awake, make demands, utter threats. How dare you live as you do? In this uncanny place? Is it because of them that I see and hear things that should not be known, should stay hidden? I feel dizzy and sick. I lie down.

I awoke again on the linen mass of patchwork cushions, the scratches burning on my arms, already red, livid and raised. One of the women was beside me, bearing iced water and a soothing cream, like an offering. "You ought to be careful in the woods, Isabelle. When it's very hot the snakes sun themselves on the path. They fall asleep and you don't notice until you step on them. You're only wearing sandals."

The cold water lacerated my throat.

There was a strange, recurring breath of wind, subtle as a parting kiss. I stand behind Jean-Michel with my arms folded and my head aching. I watch the width of his back. I can see each vertebra clearly through the light, white cotton. His skin is very dark, the hair dense on his forearms and his wrists. I watch the pale curve of his nails as he adjusts the light meters and sound levels. I see the ring he inherited from his father, the thick gold chain bracelet with his name engraved in italic gold. I have worked with Jean-Michel for five years. I have been his lover for three. I know his manner, his gestures, the inflections of his voice. To me he makes sense, adds up, every kilo of his body bearing down upon me is known territory. He is not a stupid man, nor an insensitive one. He has his own gifts, the director's eye which can make an unpleasant world appear beautiful; a trick of the light, careful editing and the scene is repainted in acceptable shades. He is famous for his documentaries on life in the coral reefs, where dangerous, exotic species, jellyfish, barracuda, electric eels, the Portuguese man-of-war, dense and brilliant in their colours, drift through clear water. He transforms dailiness into the miraculous. A Paris backstreet becomes a revelation of richness, detail, mystery. He sees things that no other man would notice. And I love him for that. I take the risk.

"Jean-Michel. There's something strange about these women. Something very odd here."

"*Je sais, mon amour*. That's why we're here – to film them."

"Oh, don't be silly. Listen. There's something else. Something much more uncanny than anything they've said or who they are."

"What do you mean?"

"They aren't always the same. They change. Or there are more of them than we think."

Jean-Michel stared at me as if I had gone mad.

"And the whole landscape seems to change. One moment it was damp and there were maize fields. Then it was hard earth underfoot and I saw nothing but sunflowers."

"Isabelle. You've spent too much time in the sun." He shook his head incredulously. "Go and look out at the view. There aren't any sunflowers. It's maize in the valley by the river."

I tried again, suddenly realizing that he would never understand. I had reached the limit of Jean-Michel's imagination.

"That's what I mean. I see maize too. But I did see sunflowers. And I can't get a grip on the house. It seems to change shape. And I know I'm not fantasizing. There really is something odd."

Jean-Michel shook his head and turned back to the black boxes and wires. "It's probably because this house is built on three sacred springs," he said, jeering at me, "all sacred to the Graces. You've been captivated by the mystic aura."

"Oh, bullshit. You won't listen, will you."

He was replaying one of the cassettes through the monitor.

Brigitte appeared, her extraordinary face full of certainty, clarity and passion. Jean-Michel gazed at her speculatively, shaking his head. We set up the halogen lamps and the cameras further down the slope under the trees, where a mass of yellow wild flowers grew in the clearing. These were *belles de nuit*, a weed, Patricia said, that she had carefully transported from the last garden where she had lived, and which grew wild now, here on the slopes. In the heat, the yellow blossoms drooped and faded, but now, in the first cool of the descending day, they freshened, opened, and lifted their heads. I did not like these flowers; to me they seemed uncanny, living things, lifting their heads, smelling blood. Jean-Michel said they were the perfect background, a stage-set ready made.

The orange cockerel followed Patricia down to the table under the trees. As Sébastien was checking the sound levels he flung back his head and began to crow. She turned to Jean-Michel and asked if he should be removed. But Jean-Michel was still enthusiastic about the sounds of the country. Unfortunately, a cockerel never crows once. At the end of a long sequence of shrieking cackles, some of which were recorded for posterity, Jean-Michel lost his temper and shouted with all the ferocity of a man who has not changed his shirt for twelve hours, "Stifle that chicken!"

"*Tais-toi*, Jogo!" said Patricia, staring at the plumed mass of insolence. The cock fluttered onto her shoulder and balanced there, his claws sinking into the fabric of her shirt. They were old, knotted claws, crinkled and ancient as fungus, delicate as lichen. She exchanged glances with the cock on her shoulder, a glance that was knowing, cunning, a shared intelligence, a conspiracy.

We interviewed Sylviane under the trees. Her words were more personal, reassuring. I felt as if a hand had been placed on my shoulder, anchoring my anxieties, making a promise. My headache ebbed. It was nearly seven o'clock when we retreated back up the slopes in search of the whisky bottle and fresh ice cubes. All in all, we had three and a half hours of film. The red brick and white stone house was hot to touch. We sat at the table by the chicken coops, now buried in shade, nibbling crisps and raisins. I gave the women the consent forms to sign. Brigitte read the disclaimer carefully. Then she said, "What guarantee can you give us that you won't distort what we said?"

"You must trust us," I said, weighing each word.

"I trust you," said Brigitte and looked straight into my face.

Jean-Michel arrived, carrying the last of the equipment. "*Faites-nous confiance,*" he said, "*nous ferons une belle image de vous.*"

"Being beautiful isn't important," said Brigitte, smiling, "it's more important to be visible and to be heard."

"I give you my word," said Jean-Michel, "I promise."

All three women stood still for a second, the birds, gathered, ranked close together. None of them were beautiful in the usual sense of the word. But that moment of stillness caught my attention. They were like the Graces, linked to one another, self-observing, self-absorbed. Brigitte and Sylviane signed the forms.

We packed up the car and said all our thank-yous and farewells. The women were warm, ordinary and good-humoured.

"Drive carefully."

"Tell us when it's coming out."

"Good luck with the filming in Spain. When is that happening?"

"Don't forget to send us a postcard, Isabelle."

"Goodbye."

"Goodbye."

"Well . . ." I said, leaning back as we pulled out on to the long straight road down the valley through the maize fields. I was terribly relieved to have escaped the disturbing mountain and its uncompromising inhabitants. "What a film it's turning out to be. The finance is in the bag. So we can edit as we like."

I looked out at the huge arched jets of the irrigation systems.

"The first breath of scandal can hit the assembled journalists at the preview. Then if there are any complaints, articles, maybe even an attempt to ban the film ... that would be good, we must persuade someone to ban the whole thing ... then we can put up a fight and be certain of a colossal audience."

I lit a cigarette, vaguely triumphant.

"Don't be so stupid, Isabelle," snapped Jean-Michel. "Do you want us all sacked? We can't use most of what we made today. Who wants to watch a film about madwomen who want to eliminate men? Lecturing normal people as if we were the perverts. It's not even interesting. I think we can have about four minutes of Brigitte if we edit her carefully – and Sylviane talking about her childhood. Look, we're doing them a favour. You can't talk like that with impunity. It sounds mad. Unhinged. And it's dangerous. Our job is to save them from their own opinions. To present them so that they can be heard. So that they don't frighten and disturb ordinary people."

I went cold. "But Jean-Michel, you promised those women. You gave your word."

"Listen. They signed the consent forms, didn't they? They can't take legal action of any kind."

"But you gave your word."

"Isabelle, we have a job to do. We decided what kind of programme we wanted to make. And we'll do that. This is going out at peak viewing time. What kind of press would we get if we plastered a pack of maniacs and radicals across the small screen?"

"But you gave your word."

"Did you want them to stop the filming and smash the camera? Women like that are perfectly capable of destroying everything we want to achieve. They aren't sensible or rational."

"They made sense to me. And you gave them your word."

"My god, shut up. You sound like a rosary."

I tightened my lip and looked out of the window. In the right-hand mirror I saw something move behind us in the maize. I went on peering into the mirror. A Renault Trafic van, cream and dark red, pulled out of the hidden lane, and followed us at a distance of two hundred metres. There were two people sitting in the front. I couldn't make out their features. They were too far away. But I knew who they were. And I knew that only I could see them.

"Jean-Michel," I screamed, terrified, clutching the dashboard, "look behind you!"

He was still very angry. He started and looked into the mirror. "*Merde*. There's nothing there. What's the matter with you?"

He increased his speed. I saw the hearse, still there in the mirror, keeping exactly the same distance between us.

"Sébastien, look!"

I turned round, desperately pointing out the back window. But all I saw was a long straight road through tall flanks of shimmering green maize, the evening light still fierce on the asphalt, the sky a darkening, aggressive blue.

"Let me out of the car. Stop the car," I shouted, "we're being followed."

Jean-Michel swore, pulled over to the right by a small bridge over the ditch and stopped the car. I was hysterical with fear. He turned towards me and slapped me hard on my left cheek. "*Arrête, tu es folle.*"

"Leave her alone," said Sébastien, getting out of the car, "there's something wrong."

I got out of the car too, and stood, shaking with fright, by the roadside.

"What's the matter, Isabelle?" Sébastien asked kindly, putting his arm around me.

"We're being followed," I screamed. He looked back down the long straight road, which was perfectly empty.

"But there's nothing there."

"There is. There is. Only you can't see them."

Sébastien looked at Jean-Michel, who was sitting in the car, smoking quickly, furious. Jean-Michel shrugged, a red spot of anger on either cheek.

"I won't go on. I can't go on. I can't." I screamed hysterically, and sat down in the dust on the edge of the ditch, crying. Sébastien leaned in at the car window.

"Listen. Go along to the next village and send a taxi or a doctor. She's sick. I'll stay with her."

Jean-Michel leaped out of the car shouting and grabbed my arm. "Get back in that car, damn you. And shut up. Stop this idiocy."

I bit his wrist hard. He let me go with a yelp of horror. I slithered down the bank and rushed into the maize; my legs and bare arms were scratched and cut as I pushed my way in, defending my face. My feet sank into the soft, turned earth. The maize was cool and wet. It had been watered that day. Far behind me I could hear Jean-Michel and Sébastien, shouting my name. I crouched down in the maize and covered my head. Gradually the voices ceased. I must have been there an hour, maybe more. I could hear nothing but the sounds of the frogs and the crickets in the evening heat, the rustle of the maize above me in the faint wind. I crept back towards the road. Of course I had lost my sense of direction and emerged further down the road from the little bridge. I paused, and looked in both directions. Far away I saw Sébastien's white shirt perched, waiting on the edge of the bridge. The car was gone. I waved frantically, very relieved, and ran down the road towards him. He stood up stiffly as he saw me coming.

"*Enfin*, Isabelle." The sweat was damp on his face. "Listen," he went on, "Jean-Michel's gone to get help. He should be back by now. He's been gone for over an hour. What on earth was the matter? Are you all right? He shouldn't have hit you."

I stood shaking in the road, unable to speak.

"What was the matter?" he repeated.

"Didn't you see anything?"

"No."

"Nothing? Really nothing?"

"No. Nothing. Nothing was following us. You were imagining things. But there was something odd. Just after Jean-Michel left, I was sitting on the bridge. And then I felt a rush of wind as if a big van was passing. And I was covered in dust. But there was no wind. The maize was quite still. It's probably a trick of the heat. That's what's affected you."

I stared at him. And then began screaming, again and again, long aching peals of horror. Sébastien grabbed my arms, which were covered in points of dried blood and scratches. He shook me violently. But I went on, screaming and screaming.

Everyone knows what happened after that. Or at least they know the bare facts. What was recorded in the newspapers. Jean-Michel's car was found upside down in the sunflowers, miles away. He was quite dead, the only mark upon him was a dark, bloody bruise on the forehead, from the blow which had splintered his skull. The engine was still, the windscreen shattered. The car was seriously damaged, but not wrecked; the equipment mostly unharmed, the boxes of taped film were intact. Sébastien identified the body. No other car was involved. And the police concluded that there were no suspicious circumstances. He had been drinking. The car had left the road.

I spent almost a month in the clinic, being treated for shock. My memories of that time are very hazy because of the drugs, but the nurses tell me that four women came, faithfully, every week, to visit me; and that one of them, older, very sunburnt, would sit close beside me, holding my hand. When I was well enough I went straight back to work. Given that I was Jean-Michel's assistant director it was not at all difficult to take over the project. I made my decision. I will keep his promise to those women. They will see themselves in all their uncanny difference. I will edit the film.

The Storm

I was elected Chairman of the Investigating Committee during the year of the great storms. That year we had a summer of stifling heat which resolved itself only in the most terrifying tempests, coming from the south-west, preceded by violent bursts of hailstones and near hurricane force winds. The high mountain Colleges were cut off for weeks by land-slides and torrents. The roads were washed away. I was frequently busy with demands from the Treasury to supervise insurance payments for storm damage. One of our own barn roofs was torn off during the last storm in August and the granaries were wrecked. I spent my days amid wailing and complaints. Our overseers began to talk in terms of curses and prophecy. They had never seen storms like these. The more superstitiously gloomy began predicting apocalypse. I said that the year was not a sufficiently magical number. Yes, it was a bad year, but that was all. Yet there were days when it was too dark to work with one lamp in my study, summer nights when I was so cold that I ordered the fire. The winds tore stone tiles from the towers, the younger boys among the initiates had nightmares and called for their mothers. Even I began to wonder if the events we had desired for centuries were at last shaping history in our remote and mountainous state.

Our College was built in the high pastures beneath a huge head of folded rock, like a giant's chin, jutting out above us. The grey stone buildings dominated the valleys curving out into the pattern of a fan below. We kept cattle, goats and poultry. We ran our own outlying farms on the low slopes and lived off the produce as most of the more prosperous Colleges do. We imported very little. I took the view that our austerity and simplicity guaranteed the stability of the state. The initiates were allowed no luxuries, but neither were the Masters. No one was spared his share of manual labour, no matter how fragile his strength. Nor, once they were established in their disciplines, were they allowed days away from their studies in the libraries, laboratories and archives. We were disciplined, secure. I never perceived our methods as cruel, but we were uncompromising. I demanded concentration, dedication and excellence from all our members. We valued each other and we valued our achievements. Looking back, I now realize that, to some extent, the landscape protected us. We were difficult to reach. There were no airports and no easy access over the mountains. We controlled the roads. We kept the world at bay. To be frank, I think it suited the outsiders to leave us in peace. We were fortified, but not belligerent. We were self-contained. And our work was priceless to them.

The first weeks of September were usually a rich, peaceful and productive time for us. The weather could normally be counted upon to remain still; sharp in the mornings, with warm, clear days, the temperature dropping fifteen, sometimes twenty degrees, at sunset. I loved this moment, when the year held its breath. But that year the vines suffered terribly and the flooding gullies caused substantial damage to our sparse agricultural land. We faced financial difficulties, if not catastrophe. We had two gentle, windy days in the second week, then the air tensed and the heat began to increase again. I sat by my window, brooding over the accounts in the murky, airless vacuum. My scholars presented their work as usual, but they were listless, or anxious. We lost our appetites and there were long silences at table. One of our musicians fell seriously ill and the infirmarian became so concerned that he sent me six-hourly bulletins. Even he blamed the weather for this mystery disease. Our spirits flagged; we sweated in stagnant vaults. The unchanging days dragged past. We made good our buildings against the inevitable storm.

On the evening of September 10th I received an urgent message from the Master of one of our southern Colleges, hidden among the white rocks and exotic pines. The roads were clear. He requested an immediate meeting. His messenger was travelling only hours ahead. He was coming in person and would be there by nightfall. All this was highly unusual. Indeed, according to our laws, only events or issues which constituted a national emergency justified this indecent alarm or the absence of a Master from his College. I checked the files. The man did have a peculiar history. He was not born into the ruling élite, but had been recruited late in the day, when he was well over seven years old, into one of our minor College schools. From these groups we usually drew and trained our overseers, managers, caretakers, civil servants. It was rare that a boy who was not one of us should rise to become a Master. I read the confidential reports. They praised his scholarship, his justice, his pastoral concern for his initiates. He was canny with money. His College never ran at a deficit. I half smiled at this. At bottom he was an overseer after all. Some of our finest scholars and scientists, whose work was incomparable, whose books and papers were pearls of great price, ran their Colleges with spectacular debts, which occasioned much passion and recrimination at the annual Management Committee. Excellence and prudence are rarely good bedfellows. It is not in my nature to speculate over coming trouble. I went out for a walk in the forest.

Under the pines the air was a little cooler, but fetid, unmoving. I paced silently through the trees, along the paths, noting the deep erosion, the banks fallen away, the tall pines ripped up, sagging against one another. At one point above the river a rockfall had almost removed the path. The foresters had laid a makeshift bridge cut from rough trunks. The sap was still golden in the splintered wood. I paused to look down at the white water crashing over the great smooth boulders, hundreds of feet below. The winter promised to be difficult. But we would survive. We had always survived. I returned to the College as the coming darkness began to breathe in the shadows and found that my expected visitor had already arrived and had demanded an audience.

I am a man who takes his time to reflect, to decide. I dislike haste and urgency. There is very little in the world that cannot wait. I sent my visitor greetings and gave orders for him to be offered wine, food and all our usual hospitality. I ate alone, in silence, and only sent for him some hours later when the house was still. I insisted upon the delay. I made him wait. The Masters meet together on annual occasions, and never alone. I sat in my library, indifferent, aloof. As he entered we made the usual bow, exchanged the usual greetings. I did not ask him to be seated. I watched him carefully. He was obsequious, cowering – and terrified. He clutched a leather box that was sealed with melted pewter. I leant back, sweating inside my state robes. The night air was breathless, stifling. Calmly, I folded my arms.

"Well?"

"Master, I have brought you a Book."

I nodded, very puzzled.

"It was written by one of my own initiates. A Novice, in fact. I have had him imprisoned. There was no hint of its contents. He was working on the history of our laws, on the potential reformation of the state. There was nothing exceptional in the project. It had been passed by the Project Committee of our College. He is one of our most gifted young scholars. Indeed, he is the best we have. None of us expected treason. And especially not from him. I still find it impossible . . ."

He had begun to ramble repetitively. I cut him short.

"What is in this seditious Book that it should occasion such exceptional excitement?"

He was very pale. He placed the leather box on the empty shining table beside me.

"We had no idea. We blame ourselves . . ." A torrent of excuses began to pour forth.

"Was the book submitted to the governing body of the College as usual?" I snapped. "Answer."

"Yes, Master."

"Did this young scholar make any attempt to conceal the contents from his authorities?"

"No, Master."

"Has he denied his Book?"

"No, Master."

"What excuses does he offer?"

"None, Master. He will not speak."

"Has he been tortured?"

"Yes, Master."

"And he still will not speak?"

"No, Master."

"Leave me."

He hesitated.

"Leave me." I lowered my voice slightly, and he backed stumbling out of the stone chamber.

I sat unmoving for many minutes. Then I took my knife out of the drawer of my desk and broke the seals. The Book was bound and presented correctly, in the manner that has been laid down for centuries. There was nothing exceptional in the dedication, the summary, the acknowledgements, nor in the table of contents. My eye skimmed the chapter headings: "On Justice", "Of Crime and Prisons", "Legitimacy", "Equality", "On Liberty", "Religion", "Concerning Slaves and Women", "On Scholarship and Truth". These were standard themes. I opened the window wide and looked out at the faint glimmers of sheet lightning illuminating the mountains. It was eerie, distant, beautiful. But there was no damp gust, no whisper of cool air. A couple of bats circled in the sticky air below. I saw the shadow of the well in the courtyard,

magnified against the great stone walls. I stretched, removed
my robes, rolled up my shirtsleeves and poured a glass of cold
water. Then I began to read.

"Can a state that is based upon slavery and force also support
the endeavour to search for truth? For this force exists not as
a last resort for our security, but as a present menace; to
dissuade and prevent our slaves – and ourselves – from seeking
freedom. Freedom is the prerequisite for our endless voyage
towards knowledge and truth. How can we, as a male-only
ruling élite, also claim to be defending and protecting our
women, whom we have reduced to a category that is less than
human? We cannot pretend to have faith in a religion which
places women and men as equals in the sight of God and
deny women access to all our privileges. Our women are
deliberately kept illiterate, like breeding cattle; their only func-
tion being to reproduce the ruling-class élite. What we have
defined as knowledge and as truth is the prerogative of a
privileged few. But there are other knowledges and other
truths. How can we speak of absolute ethics when our laws
operate only through violence, not consent? We claim to be
the guardians of our people, but we cannot know if we have
their consent. They have never been consulted. We continue
to hold power, not because we are the custodians of our
people's welfare, but because it is in our interests to do so.
We benefit from our position in practical, tangible ways. Our
hierarchy ensures that each group in the pyramid only remains
in place and holds the scant privileges to which they are
entitled by ensuring the oppression of the group below them.
Thus each betrays the other, but always to our advantage. At
the base of this pyramid is the most helpless, disadvantaged
group of all, the women. Who are responsible for most of our
agriculture, who rear our animals, plant our crops, produce
our sons. They dread bearing daughters, the majority of whom
will be slaughtered at birth. We do not know how many of
our women have killed themselves rather than live on as

slaves, or been butchered throughout history in the numerous uprisings which exist only as folklore, and are never recorded in the annals of the state. But there is an historical memory that exists outside archives and documents, a memory that lives in songs, proverbs, poetry, myths, apparently harmless little stories – and in the writing on our prison walls. We have only to learn how to read these languages to understand that the acquiescent silence of our people has never been that of consent. Our history, our knowledge, our scholarship, is a web of arrogance and lies. We produce patterns of tyranny to offer to an ugly world. Our God looms over us, a monster in our own image. We have no natural right to govern as we do. We have sewn the garments of cruelty and made these the habit of our days. We prize sadism and call it the practice of austerity. Our methods are neither just, nor justifiable. We reward cowardice, conformism and meretricious frauds. Even among ourselves there is no freedom to love, to think, and to speculate against possibility. Our desires are moulded by the state, which punishes difference with calculated ruthlessness. To speak of liberty, here within this system which we dispraise at peril of our lives, is empty meaningless cant. We are comfortable, privileged, intellectual slaves, slaves to an idea of excellence that is hollow, a relic adrift in history. We will not survive; neither as a state nor as isolated intellectual communities, and we do not deserve to survive. Our corruption is visible, evident. We are now living – arrogant, complacent, foolish – in the still eye of the coming storm."

I read on and on into the night, my bones stiffening. The glass of cold water remained untouched beside me. As first light shimmered in the courtyard below I stood up and knew that I had aged ten years in one night. I leaned over, ungainly, insecure, to blow out the lamp, so that my servant would not see the light under the door. Then I stood, silent and reflective, beside the open window. I could not immediately grasp what was required. I could not understand what it was that I would have to do. The light thickened outside. I felt the sun on the tips of the mountain pines long before I saw the massive rising of the day. I heard the rattle of buckets by the pumps. The College was already stirring. All the usual sounds, which I had heard every day for nearly fifty years, unfolded throughout the buildings, disciplined, secure. I turned back into my shadowy stone chamber and replaced the Book in its leather case. The way was clear before me.

As Grand Master of the Colleges I had the power to call us all together. But that would give the Book too much credence. Our meeting for that year had already taken place in May. There had been nothing untoward, only the usual financial wrangles and quarrels over leave of absence from the country. I had been elected Chairman of the Investigating Committee, which I always attended in any case on account of my higher office. The Committee consisted of the seven Masters who governed the wealthiest and most powerful Colleges. We met every two months, but not during the most savage winter seasons when the roads were impassable. I had made my decision. I summoned my Deputy, who came at once, surprised and curious, for my colleague's sudden arrival had been whispered through all the corridors and cells. I nodded as he bowed, and said curtly, "Call an extraordinary meeting of the Investigating Committee at the Castle in three days' time. See that all the Masters are summoned. We will need extra guards and scribes. I will set out at midday. You will hold office in my absence. Leave me now."

He scuttled out of the room, twitching with excitement. I locked all the doors and went to bed.

The Castle is an enormous dilapidated keep over a day's trek above our College. In the Middle Ages it was a fortress that had preserved the community during the wars. Later it had served as a prison. Now that we were able to reach our final decisions much more rapidly we had no need to leave dissenters languishing in dungeons. The Castle had therefore fallen into disrepair. Parts of it were shut up. One of our overseers informed me that the gatehouse roof had been ripped off during the recent storms. I had not considered repairs a priority. I regretted my decision at once when I saw the up-ended rafters jutting above the walls through the strange windless white light of the late afternoon. We were the first to arrive. All the rooms smelt musty and damp. I sent our people scurrying through the old kitchens, down the staircases, into the stables. We are used to austerity, but even I concluded that large parts of the building were no longer habitable. The Council Chamber tapestries were rotten and moth-eaten, the enamel was chipped on the floor tiles. A heap of dead birds lay in the ashes of the huge open fireplace. Cobwebs and green mould decorated the great oak trestle tables and benches. The task before us was discouraging. I left them to their work, and locked myself away in the tower with the Book, which had never left my presence since it had been put into my hands.

Too many eyes had already seen what was written there. I calculated that the five members of the Southern College's governing body as well as the Master must have seen the final text. Or some part of it at least. The Novices regularly presented their work, to colleagues and to members of other Colleges. Yet no whisper of this Book had ever reached my spies. I had checked every regular filed report. The Novice's name was unknown to me. His file was clean. There were simply records of excellence, prizes for achievements. The only thing that was odd was that he had demanded to keep his mother's name. Usually, upon entering the College, the boys all choose another name, the sign of their passage into manhood and into our ranks. Very few ever retain any links with the women, who are soon cast off and forgotten. That is our way and we have always preferred that it should be so.

I now saw the consequence and significance of even so tiny a breach in the armour of our customs and practices. This single eccentricity which, in my perusal of the novitiate files I had certainly overlooked, now glared back from the page, sinister with implications. I cracked my knuckles in irritation; then set about my task of summarizing the Book into a form that would sufficiently alarm and enrage the Investigating Committee so that this young man's death and the destruction of every scrap of writing he had ever produced were a foregone conclusion. At all costs neither the raw content of his arguments, nor the abrasive power of his rhetoric should escape from my grasp. My tone was brutal, factual and cold. Nothing extenuate, nor set down aught in malice. But it was many hours later before I leant back, satisfied with my text. I was now curious to meet this young man, whose death warrant I had sealed.

He was transferred to the old prison as soon as he arrived. I was informed, of course, but I suppressed my curiosity. There is very little in the world that cannot wait. By the evening of the third day all the Masters had arrived. Some had travelled alone across great distances. The atmosphere in the Castle was electric with rumours. The heat was unbearable. We were all in bad tempers and very uncomfortable. I called the first session in the Council Chamber at dawn on the following day.

As we faced one another I looked carefully into each old, lined, locked face. These were the men in whom I had placed my trust. These were the Masters who controlled the state. They sat silent, waiting, most of them uncannily still, with their eyes half closed. They were dangerous as serpents and soft as doves. I gazed at each man in turn, weighing my suspicions, my fears. Then, without a flicker of acknowledgement that what I was doing was extraordinary and without raising my voice I addressed our attendants, scribes and recorders, who were waiting expectantly.

"Leave us. Lock up the doors. No one is to leave the building."

There was a rustle of surprise and alarm as they withdrew from the Council Chamber. None of the Masters moved. I suddenly realized what they expected. One of them stood accused. I rose.

"No, my friends, I have not brought you here to spread suspicion and fear. We all stand accused. The material I am about to present to you was produced by one of our number. He passed all his initiate exams with honours and awards. Everyone here must have seen his work at one time or another. And I had no indication of any doubts or questions from any one of you."

I paused. Then spoke very quietly. "A case of heresy as articulate and as dangerous as this cannot have sprung up overnight. This Book took years to write. Therefore we all stand accused."

I paused again, so that my words would take effect. These men were the lords and owners of their faces. They made no sign. I sighed slightly, balanced my weight, and began to speak. The great bars of light, solid with swirling dust, traversed the Chamber. Gradually, as the Book took shape before them, the Masters tensed. There were no outbursts or exclamations. Each period was greeted in silence. But the quality of the silence began to change. Expectation was transformed into incredulity, and finally, as I had calculated, into anger and alarm. When I had reseated myself, they began to stir. The eldest among them, a man who was also my senior, spoke first.

"The Southern College must be obliterated as swiftly as possible," he said quietly, "and in this case neither the slaves nor the women should be permitted to live."

A faint murmuring began. And then there were many questions.

"Can we be certain that there are no other extant copies of this Book?"

"Is the writer still living?"

"He must appear before us at dawn tomorrow."

"Is that necessary? Surely we have heard enough?"

"The Master of the Southern College was not born into our number. The Rule has not been followed."

"Have we any files on any other members of that College?"

"Are the records of their movements available?"

"When was this project passed by their governing body?"

The answer to this question – that it had been passed four years previously – occasioned the nearest thing to panic that I had ever observed among the Masters. They all looked at me directly and the eldest folded his arms. We were of one mind on the need for ruthlessness and rapidity, but a new sensation assailed us all: the fear that we were already too late. How had it come about that no one had suspected the contents of the Book? That this young scholar had remained unsupervised? That the Book had not been checked, scrutinized, during the process of its making? But one central mystery haunted all our minds and I put that question into words.

"Why was this Book submitted to the College to be published? We are not dealing with an inferior underground publication. It came to our notice only through the usual procedures. This young madman sought our imprimatur."

There was a dreadful pause.

"He must testify to this Committee," I said carefully, "we must judge for ourselves."

No one offered an opinion. I closed the session and the Masters dispersed. Not one spoke to the others. As was our custom.

Late that afternoon when the heat had ebbed I descended the steps on the outer walls to the prison. I noticed the foliage growing in the cracks, the lichen covering the broken stones. Everywhere I saw decrepitude and decay. We were already inhabiting the ruins of our power, we were ghosts in our own past. I paused at the rusted outer gates, at the bottom of the first long flight and stood, gazing back up at the block of bright white light far above me. Then I decided to do something extraordinary. I wanted to find myself equal even to this meeting. I turned to the guard who was struggling with the unyielding locks.

"Bring him up into the light. I will take him with me into the forest."

The guard stared at me for a second. He was trained to obey. "Yes, Master" was all he said.

And so I waited in the bright white light for the boy who had written the Book.

As he paused, blinking, on the top step, stumbling in his fetters, I had a long moment in which to stare, unobserved, at his face. He was tall, slenderly built, almost fragile, with long transparent hands. He looked helpless; an unlikely, indecisive scholar, neither a conspirator nor a radical. I did not have a muscular hero standing before me, but an intellectual, unmistakably one of our number, the sign of our Order of Masters tattooed on his wrist. His hair was ash-blond and uncut, tied back with a dirty string. I had examined countless other young men whom he resembled exactly. The situation was becoming increasingly unbelievable.

"Set him free," I ordered the guard.

The boy staggered free of the fetters and turned to peer at the face behind my voice. He recognized me at once. "Master," he said, automatically making the obligatory bow.

"Can you walk?"

He tried a few steps towards me.

"I see you can. Follow me."

And I walked away towards the gatehouse and into the forest.

The Novices always follow their Masters. My suspicions were confirmed. He was trained in the prescribed manner. I had nothing to fear. Once we were well beyond the Castle I indicated that he should walk beside me. He limped, and appeared to be in pain. I walked slowly for a while and then stopped under the cool of the pines. Neither of us had spoken. He slumped down at my feet against a pile of cut logs, still sticky with sap. I stood a little behind him, watching his exhausted face.

"I wish to ask you a few questions," I said calmly.

He said nothing. I looked at the raw, seeping burns on his arms and ankles and pursed my lips. I do not expect our torturers to leave marks on their subjects. This was very unprofessional.

"Why did you submit the Book to your governing body?"

"I thought it was good enough to be published."

"You cannot have been so naïve."

"I was."

"Was it entirely your own work?"

"Yes."

"How long have you held the opinions expressed in your Book?"

"I must have felt them. Always. They developed as I wrote."

"How many other scholars saw the Book?"

"No one. I presented other work. I thought it was too dangerous. That I would be stopped before I had finished."

"Are there any other copies?"

"No."

"Do you have notes, drafts?"

"Yes. They were all in my cell. I imagine they have already been burnt."

"Have you written anything else?"

"Nothing that was not in my cell. All my other work on our laws has already been presented in public."

"Did you expect to be arrested for writing this Book?"

"Yes. No. That is – I thought I might be."

"Were you afraid?" I asked softly.

"Yes."

"Why did you do it?"

"I had to."

"Why?"

He looked up at me. His eyes were black with pain and tears. "Because it's the truth."

I turned away a little, then paused to look at him, my face in shadow. He was extraordinarily young.

"Do you know what you're risking?"

"Yes," he said simply, turning and looking straight into my face.

"I don't think that you do."

He shrugged.

"We couldn't let you go, you know. It's not a question of reprimanding you for naïveté and foolishness, then sending you back to your College."

He huddled at my feet, quite still, listening carefully. I measured out my words.

"I cannot let you leave here. Unless you recant."

His chin came up. "No."

There was all the courage and folly of youth in his emphasis. Then I took the greater risk. The murky white light was in his eyes as he turned away from me. I put my hand on his shoulder.

"It is a formula. You must understand me. Recant and I will burn your Book."

He shook himself free of me. "You'll have to burn me too."

I sighed, suddenly exhausted and old. "It may come to that," I said heavily.

That night I could not sleep. I paced my empty, filthy chamber, obsessed with the simplicity of his answers, tormented by the knowledge that he was not lying, but also by the conviction that this Book could not have been written by an innocent, unaware of his actions. The heat was intolerable. I lay down, got up, wandered back and forth between my bed and the open window, which sagged in its frame against the wall. Finally I gave way, dressed and, taking up the lantern, strode away down the dusty, empty staircases to the prison on the outer walls. I could no longer wait. I had to be certain.

I nodded to the guard, who rose at once on hearing my

step, but I did not speak. I could not trust my own voice. I simply indicated the great lock and the rusted bars. He began to unbarricade the cells, fumbling with the huge old keys. Inside, the damp seeped sweating from the great slate flagstones. Clumps of moss flourished on the walls, the hideous chill of unwashed bodies and the stench of faeces haunted the passage. I tapped my way after the guard, who held up the lantern to guide my steps into the dark. We found the young scholar asleep on a bench in his cell, a blanket flung round his shoulders, his legs coiled up, fragile as a new foetus. I stood watching him as the guard laboriously undid the festoons of ancient chains which hung around the bars of his cage. The boy was exhausted and did not stir.

"Shall I wake him for you, Master?" mumbled the guard.

"No. Leave us. Lock the gates behind you. I'll call you when I'm ready."

I stepped into the narrow coffin space, lifting the lantern into a niche in the stones. The walls were covered in detached hieroglyphics, the last words of all the thousands of prisoners who had passed into the vaults. I stood there staring at this undeciphered writing on the wall, like a prophet who has missed his calling. It remained opaque to me. I looked down at the face of the unconscious boy. The dark rings of sleeplessness were curving beneath his eyes. His hair lay tangled across his forehead. He had been crying. I stooped over him and touched his cheek. It was olive – smooth, as soft as that of a young child. I gazed at him with terrible compassion. But I would not forget what it was that I had come to do. He awoke with a start and covered his eyes; then gawped unseeing into my face.

"Master," he cried out at last.

"Be calm. Be quiet. You won't be harmed."

I sat down on the bench beside him. He recoiled against the wall. We stared at one another in the flickering light. The straw crunched dully under my feet. His tear-stained face was like a bruise.

"Why have you come? Do the Committee want me to testify? Now? In the night?"

"No. That will be tomorrow. Save your strength. I've come to demand a little clarification from you."

He tensed, an animal crouched and at bay.

"Was the Book entirely your own work?"

"You've asked me that."

"I'm asking again."

"I've told you. I wasn't lying."

"Then it was your hand only."

"Yes."

Suddenly I saw through the subtlety of his evasions and seized his shoulders, my hands tight as clamps.

"Yes, your hand only. But you were not the sole source. There are more of you. How many? Who are your collaborators?"

His face was white, set against me. I was shaking with anger.

"I will burn your College into cinders. Every barn, every Book, every stone."

"Burn the world," he whispered savagely. "You cannot unwrite my words. They are written in your brain."

I flung him back onto the bench. His temple cracked against the wall. I slapped his face again and again, until his blood spattered my hands. I was beside myself. I punched him with all my force, in the face, in the chest. He offered no resistance, simply shrank back, attempting to cover his head. I stopped short, breathing heavily. Minutes passed in a terrible heaving silence. Neither of us moved. I looked up. He was watching me.

Was he afraid? Yes, but the fear was a long way back in his eyes. There was something else, closer. He was watching not only my face, but my hands. And in that concentrated gaze, masked by sheets of blood, covering the left side of his face, was a stillness, a knowing calculation. Then I knew that I was dealing not with an idealistic Novice but with an alien, a revolutionary, a mind that had judged the risks. And was playing to win.

I stared at him, tingling with shock. The courageous anger, his articulacy, those passionate words, all this marked him out as one of us, but this sudden stillness, this moment of watching, calculating my movements, my gestures, I had seen only among the animals – *and among the women.* We stared at one another, his face a mixture of terror and defiance, while I sat slumped, horrified and appalled.

I put my head in my hands, feeling utterly lost. I had beaten this child unjustly, for writing down what I had forbidden myself even to think. But in his cunning he knew that I too could have written the Book. I had only myself to blame. I was both the betrayer and the betrayed.

My body ached. Beyond the bars across the tiny slit window above us, I saw the sky turning to blue, then to grey. In an hour it would be dawn. The child beside me, blood drying on his cheeks and his habit, sat frozen, unmoving. I turned to stare at him again. My eyes rested upon his face. He flinched.

"Forgive me," I said softly.

He shrank away.

"This is not some new trick," I said, "forgive me for striking you. I had no right to do so."

He drew his knees up to his chin, and pulled the blanket round him, his split lip curling in scorn. "You can do exactly as you please," he said, "you are the Master."

But I would not be drawn again.

"Listen," I said at last, "I think I understand you. Or at least I know better who you are. I also know that it is no use asking you to trust me. You never will. You know that I can have you killed. I can kill you myself – or I can set you free. Today you must testify to the Committee. It is up to you what you say, how you defend yourself. Speak the truth. Not the whole truth. But some part of the truth. And I will order the Committee to set you free."

The boy froze.

"Yes. I know. You suspect me. You think I will have the guards waiting for you in the forest. I am not so crude. But you must leave the country. By tomorrow night I want to be certain that you have covered more than half the distance on your way to the frontier. In three days I want news that you have escaped into exile. I will see that you are provided with money, food and transport. You never will trust what I say. But this time – take note of what I do."

I had regained my composure and my strength. I was decided. I turned towards him and looked intently into his battered face, so that I would remember every line and shade through all the years to come.

"Take note of what I do," I said again. This time the menace was unmasked. He heard the threat. But I doubt if he understood. I banged my stick against the bars to call the guard, never taking my eyes off his face. This terrible honesty would remain between us, and between us alone, for ever. There had been too many betrayals.

The sky was darkening rapidly over the mountains in the south-west. I negotiated each one of the stone steps with all the temerity and caution of a man twice my age. The boy was standing, hooded and waiting, by the gatehouse. The guard was already opening the bolts and the grille, making ready for our prisoner to depart. We faced one another for the last time. I could not find the words, so I took refuge in one final masquerade. Stripping the seal ring from my little finger I put it into his hand. His fingers were clammy, chilled and shut. I prised them open, then folded them back over the ring.

"This is your right of passage. If you should encounter any difficulties then you may draw upon my authority. Go now. God bless you."

I took him in my arms. Whatever the truth of this tense, unyielding body which resisted my embrace, I knew that I was sending forth one tiny fragment of pure freedom which had defeated us. I drew back. He did not speak, but limped rapidly away and passed through the gate like a shadow. I watched him vanish into the forest. Far away we heard the first soft mutter of the coming storm. I gave orders to secure all the shutters and doors; then returned to the Council Chamber.

The Investigating Committee were no longer silent. They were muttering openly against the perversity of my decisions. This young scholar was clearly a dangerous man. They had been scandalized both by his fearlessness and by my calm. Several were of the opinion that he should already have been executed. I stood before them and grasped the edge of the oak table to steady myself. I laid out my reasoning point by point. As I harangued the mutinous Committee the distant glamour of the thunder hastened towards us. I heard myself shouting into the crackling electric air.

"The Book is written. It did not arise from one single brain. This courageous fool is not alone. This Book will be written again and again and again. If we execute him some other hand will take up the pen. Print the Book. Only by letting this loose with the stamp of our approval can we contain its power. Burn this Book and the ashes will re-form within a year. Are you all mad? Are we to purge our monasteries and Colleges of every hot-headed idealist that ever looked into a library? Hold weekly interrogations? Inspect every scrap of manuscript? We can slaughter this Book with the precision of cobras if we give our imprimatur. It will be hailed as radical thinking originating from our Committee. We will publish equally extraordinary refutations. In a year or two we can silence the debate. Hear me now, Masters."

I slammed my hand down upon the seals. A gigantic jagged line of fork lightning sliced across the great windows of the Council Chamber. Voices were raised against me on all sides. In the last seconds of clarity I had left before the storm broke over us I shouted out, "*Nihil obstat, imprimatur.*"

Then we could hear nothing but the stone vault fractured

with echoes of the speaking thunder. The lamps went out. The room was in uproar. We were left alone with the storm.

The Glass Porch

A married woman decided to leave her husband. She told him about her decision and how she had arrived at her conclusions one Sunday morning over breakfast. Her husband was eating toast in his pyjamas. He went on covering sheets of wholemeal in marmalade as she advanced various explanations, but no compromising excuses.

All right, he said, when she had finished, and how do you propose to support yourself? She stared at him blankly. Face facts, he said, swallowing a mouthful of sugary tea. You do two hours a week of voluntary marriage guidance counselling. And given what you've just been telling me, I hope to God you only listen. You do four hours at the Old People's Home for which you are paid £1.30 an hour. You don't earn a penny for the Red Cross evenings, nor for the young drug addicts' rehabilitation scheme. So your entire weekly income amounts to £5.20. I doubt that would even cover your bus fares. Are you going to tramp down to Women's Aid and say that I've beaten you? You'll have to muster up a few bruises. I suppose you could always fling yourself downstairs. Or are you going to potter off to Social Security and tell them that I crushed your spirit? Sounds poetic, but a bit unrealistic. And I'm not moving out of here just to suit you. You could always go and stay with your sister until you've sorted out that muddle in your head. Mind you, she couldn't even keep you in handkerchiefs. And anyway, you always say she drives you mad with her complaining. Well, why don't you go to your

sister's for a week, think it all over and come back next Friday?
I can eat at the canteen.

He paused. I'll give you the money for the train fare, he
said peaceably.

But I need, I desire . . . she thought.

You amount to nothing, he said.

She went upstairs to pack.

He got up to take a bath.

The water was steaming as it belched out of the tap in rushing
jerks. He turned the cold tap on as well. He selected two
clean towels out of the airing cupboard and added a little
Badedas to the incoherent flow. The viscous green trickle
began to dissolve into foam, surging round the whirlpools of
hot and cold water. He went in search of his transistor with
the intention of listening to "The Archers Omnibus" He
hummed a little tune. The bath was full of foam. He sat
down on the lavatory, speculatively. All the familiar objects
settled down around him to offer encouragement. His electric
razor snuggled into its case, the flannels folded themselves
into squares, a small pile of unused scented soaps rearranged
itself into the colours of the rainbow, declaring the importance
of simple beauties in domestic surroundings. His toothbrush
pushed hers to the other side of the glass. A long and
satisfying turd slid out of his arse. He eased his buttocks more
comfortably against the bowl and looked down at his cock,
uncircumcised, neatly shrivelled, hanging into the void. His
shit smelled of casual victory. The lavatory paper unrolled
towards him in a gesture of comradely confidence. He helped
himself to more squares then he would usually use. He felt
he deserved it. The bath filled with scented foam. Even the
soft, gurgling flush of the cistern as he touched the chrome
seemed to shake his hand in congratulation. He lowered his
backside gently into the bath. Those first few moments in a
hot bath, as the night melts away and the water caresses your
skin, are always sensual, masterly, reassuring. He leaned back,

letting the foam rise up to his ears and sighed with pleasure. He closed his eyes.

She sat on the edge of the bed, her skirt pulled well down over her knees, her eyes fixed on the roses in the wallpaper. The pattern unfolded endlessly across the wall. The roses smelt of putrefaction. She watched the flowers fading, splaying open in thick shafts of sunlight. The house was beginning to curl up and die. In a panic she pulled her small suitcase out of the wardrobe. Then there was a moment of terrible hesitation as she realized that the dresses hanging in the cupboard had begun to rot. They smelt of mushrooms and horse shit. She slammed the door shut and rushed at the chest of drawers. Her vests, underwear and nylon slips were still untainted. Quickly she flung handfuls of brassières, suspender belts, nylon stockings, carefully darned at the toes, into the bag. Two blouses in the drawer beneath could still be salvaged, but the slow, sweet odour of decomposition had already touched all her cardigans and pullovers. She fled from the room and plunged downstairs. It was becoming more important to escape from the house than to plunder its spoils. She risked the kitchen.

At first glance all was well. The surfaces were wiped clean, the breakfast dishes neatly stacked; but as she stared mistrustfully at the white and cream cupboards she saw a slow brown stain running down one of the doors. A movement startled her. There was something stirring inside the washing machine. She froze. Slowly, the metal circle turned over, once, twice, stopped. She looked around desperately. Every surface was covered in old food, rotten vegetables, plates of Chinese takeaway, abandoned, weeks old, bottles of beer, flat, half-drunk, saucepans filled with inedible, hideous grease, frying pans thick with congealed and rotting sausages. An ashtray overflowing with fag ends stood next to an evil-smelling pot of raspberry jam. The odours mounted up like a pyramid, one upon the other. She clapped her hand to her mouth and backed out of the door. Clearly there was very little time left.

Upstairs, he sank peacefully under the warm foam and then reached for the shampoo. His hair was streaked with grey, but still thick. He squeezed a soggy blob of Wash and Go onto his left hand and gently began to massage his dandruff. His toes rose out of the steam on either side of the taps; a corn bulged on the side of his instep. He surveyed the yellow lump critically. These things happen. He would apply another of those pink corn plasters he had in the medicine cabinet. In time it would drop off.

She went through the pockets of his jacket and helped herself to the fifty pounds left in his wallet after the weekend shopping. Then she took out the credit card and the cheque book. She did not feel safe in the hallway. On the table by the phone there was a pile of used Kleenex which had not been there half an hour before. There was a half-eaten biscuit and a mass of elderly crumbs. She swept up his car keys and risked putting on her old corduroy coat. She had had this coat for years, long before her marriage. It was now her gardening coat, and smelt not of stealthy decomposition but of fresh, green earth. She paused, reinhabiting the coat. One button was missing. Here were her gardening gloves, worn through at the tips, stuffed into the pocket. She put them on. Handbag. Small bag. She burst into the sitting-room and snatched her favourite cassettes out of the black semi-circular rack where her husband stored them all in alphabetical order. The sitting-room was littered with crisp packets, Coca-Cola cans and newspapers everywhere, on the floor, on the tables, stuffed into the cracks of the armchairs. The cushions sagged greasily onto the carpet. She screwed her eyes to slits and snatched back her music; nothing but dance music, tangos, rumbas, waltzes, galliards, can-cans, minuets, flamenco, Gay Gordons, country and western, the unadulterated polka. She rammed the music into her bag. The song rang in her head like a mantra: You should see me dance the polka, you should see me cover the ground, you should see my coat-tails flying, as I whirl my partner round. She bolted out of the room.

She stood before the front door wearing her gardening clothes, carrying nothing but her handbag and a small suitcase.

The keys were hanging from the lock on the front door of the house.

The door was locked.

She let herself silently out of the house and shut the door carefully behind her. The Yale clicked into place.

She stood inside the glass porch with the keys in her hand. She looked at the keys. They were her husband's keys. She flung them back through the letter box as if she had been burned.

The glass porch ran the length of the house. It was built on the south side and caught all the sun. They kept the living-room curtains pulled shut on hot days, to keep out the heat. There were no geraniums or cacti in the porch. She had wanted to have flowering plants, so that the porch would have been a mass of colour and greenery. He had told her that she couldn't. The glass porch was tiled and bare. She swept the tiles clean every day. At the end of the glass porch was another door, the outside door, the door which led down the garden path by the side of the house past the garage. The outside door was also made of glass, but reinforced glass, glass melted into a strong wire grille, thick, twisted wire to discourage burglars.

And the outside door was always kept locked. She had just slid the keys through the letter box. They were now lying splayed out upon a filthy, flowered carpet.

She was therefore imprisoned within the glass porch.

She stood shaking in the warm bare space, long, clean, unchanging, like a vaginal canal. She tried the outside door, knowing that it was locked. The handle was warm to the touch. She took a deep breath and walked back to the front door. This was a Victorian door in patterned coloured glass, ovals, squares, neat whirling patterns in yellow, burnt red and cobalt blue. The lead divisions, smooth and sure as a draughtsman's lines, maintained the whole. She leaned against the heavy Victorian door. It was firmly locked. She felt the glass gathering heat and force.

Upstairs, he scrubbed his chest with a loofah she had bought at the Body Shop, then sank back, pink, hairy and content. He turned on the radio and watched a little blob of foam sliding down the sticky grille of the transistor. The last hymn of the morning service from St Margaret's, County Antrim, poured forth.

She prowled the length of the porch like a panther, carrying her bags. She looked utterly ridiculous.

He sang along with the last verse of the hymn: Praise, my soul, the King of Heaven. They used to sing that at school.

She put down her bags.

He turned on the hot tap.

Suddenly she took off one shoe, and, holding it ferociously by the toe, attacked the marvellous curling glass swirls with her heel. The lead lines gave way as if they had only been pencil marks, the glass fractured and split. She struck and struck, again and again. Huge fragments, tiny splinters, went hurtling into the front hall, covering the oily yellow roses that were rotting on the floor. She yelled in triumph. The entire lead frame shivered and gave way. She recoiled, jubilant, from the gaping hole that hung senseless like a bleeding mouth with all the teeth knocked out. She swung round and, gathering all her force, attacked the gleaming panes which revealed the stately process of lawns, dug beds and raked gravel. The garden shattered into a thousand elegant diamonds and crumbled before her. Now she knew the absolute pleasure of destruction. Pane after pane shivered and collapsed before her force. Her shining, flaying heels – for she had now removed both her shoes – created huge, circling spider patterns with a bullet hole in the centre of the vibrating cracks. She smashed the glass outwards, away from herself, but inevitably great flying splinters cascaded onto the tiles of the porch. No matter, she was untouchable. Miraculously, her stockinged feet remained undamaged, uncut. She stretched upwards, moving back towards the outside door, and flung herself against the smooth clear sheets of roofing glass which began to pour down, translucent, shining, deadly, solid masses of glass rain.

In his terror he knocks the transistor into the water. The entire house is shaking, heaving like a woman in labour. Great chunks of glass are falling into the bath; the fluffy blue mat which he had shaken out, not half an hour before, is covered in broken splinters and glass dust. The mirror above the basin has great jagged cracks across the surface. Shards of broken glass are appearing everywhere in the bathroom, on the floor, in the basin, in the lavatory, in the soap dish, on the flannels, all over the window ledge and the wooden shelf with his electric razor in its smooth black case, now covered with a broken mass of glass.

Her right arm strikes, again and again, and with each magnificent, exuberant blow her cup overflows in a mighty torrent of dancing joy.

Upstairs, a man stands, naked and preposterous as St Sébastien. With every move his skin is pierced and bleeding. A thousand tiny flecks of blood are covering his body, every wound a puncture from the flying glass. The blood runs down into the bath, discolouring the foam.

Downstairs, a woman pauses to adjust her coat and scarf. She puts on her shoes. She dusts the splinters from her bag with her gardening gloves. A faint tinkle of fragments falls from the towel rail. Then she steps out through the empty frames of the ruined porch into pure light and fresh, clean autumn air.

Gramsci and the Sparrow

We were about to leave the house when the cat flap flew open and Gramsci – grey and white with extraordinary orange eyes, eyes that were now vast, black, predatory with satisfaction – came hurtling through with a mass of squeaking feathers in his jaws. We stood, our files, books and notes descending in armfuls, shrieking no, no, no, no, no. We must speak about freedom. We have read many optimistic and fiery books. We are confronting a massacre. The sparrow flew out of the cat's mouth, flapped twice and collapsed. Gramsci pounced. We dropped every book and paper and flung ourselves over furniture, against bookshelves, behind televisions, into the foliage of potted plants. The room became a heap of wreckage, fur and feathers. Repeated shouts echoed like slogans: SHUT THAT CAT FLAP! CUT HIM OFF AT THE STAIRS! IS IT DEAD YET? OMIGOD, I'M TERRIFIED OF DEATH! DROP IT, GRAMSCI, YOU MURDERING BASTARD!

The scene resolved into a scowling grey and white cat sitting resentfully on the window sill, one woman gathering up books and trembling with a recently acquired bird phobia, and the other woman righteously indignant, with a tiny sparrow up her sleeve, its small heart bursting. We address one another on the right to die in security, dignity and peace. We prepare a box in a darkened room. Satisfied with our speeches and decisions, we left devouring nature alone with the tiny bird and sped away to lecture on the freedom of women.

We returned hours later, psychologically prepared to bury the dead. Gramsci was extended along the fence, still sulking. As we entered the house he half-closed his eyes, his head turned away in contempt. We had stolen the pleasure of the kill. We had refused his gift. I tiptoed into the darkened room and peered into the box.

What had I expected to see? A diminished tuft of feathers, two stiff curled legs and an eye smoky in death. Instead, a small cheeky bird, steady on its feet, turned its head to one side, and looked up at me.

We kissed one another passionately, snatched up the box and roared off to the vet.

The vet was very old, with half-moon glasses and liver-spotted hands. "Be prepared," he said, accepting the box, "they always die." I agreed to ring him up after four o'clock.

"Don't get your hopes up," said my friend, as I pounded the telephone. She sat staring at Gramsci who was chewing the stems of blown tulips in the raised brick flower bed by the back window.

"Ah, your sparrow," I heard the vet's voice, full of pleasure, "he made a full recovery. And he was set free."

Aria Nova

Let me tell you about the briefest and most extraordinary love affair I ever had. Everything about the incident was original, peculiar, bizarre. It was so unexpected. I was not looking for trouble, so to speak. Indeed, I was on my way home after an interview for a university post, and I was in a state of panic because I had accepted the job. I was also quite convinced that I had made a terrible mistake. But it was too late to withdraw my consent. A bleak mountainous future, lost in the northern provinces, stretched before me. I sat on the train thinking about driving rain, damp mornings in congealed mist, morose colleagues going through horrific divorce proceedings and depressed, debt-ridden students. I hardly noticed the summer fields dancing past. The train reached Paris at midday.

I have good friends in Paris. I have the keys to their flat. I let myself into the dark, shuttered space; tiny galley kitchen, a bathroom narrow as a dagger's blade, a soft interior full of technology and opulent plants. I took off my shoes and burst into tears, facing a precipice of unavoidable disaster. Every evil is much worse imagined. I am cursed with a vivid imagination. Wailing gave way to sniffing gulps in due course and I began to take note of the sounds outside: pigeons on the window sill, shitting among the geraniums, the sound of smashing glass in the bottle bank, a quarrel in Arabic. I shuffled sideways into the bathroom and washed my face. My friends have one of those idiotic theatrical mirrors surrounded by a string of white bulbs, vicious as parsnips, which add ten years to your age. I put my tongue out at my own reflection. Then I rammed half the Kleenex box down the lavatory. No matter how conscientious they are about cleaning that sinister yellow bowl, it always smells of urine and disease. They have a barrage of ozone-friendly aerosols positioned suggestively on the edge of the shower. None of them are effective. I watched the Kleenex vanish. My tears swirled away into the Paris sewers. I sat down to take stock of my progress so far.

All right, so the future was not promising. But at least it was going to be paid for by a state institution. Money is a great consolation in times of sorrow. So I thought about money. Solitary nights on a lonely mountain were not immediately appetizing either, but I would buy a video and watch homoerotic forties war films where the men fall into one another's arms, declare themselves and then die. There was one film I remembered, set on a very slowly sinking battleship full of gaping holes, in which the entire cast, their shirts unbuttoned to the waist, died one by one, moaning against the captain's manly chest. I'm surprised it got past the British Board of Film Censors with a "U" certificate. I've seen it three times. So the winter evenings were more or less taken care of, or at least, their terrifying length was halved. Reading books, writing lectures, and marking essays would fill up the rest of the time. I turned my thoughts to food. If you have lived in France for years, the prospect of being separated from your favourite restaurant and your friends' kitchens is harrowing. The vision of the British supermarket and pre-packaged, chemically enhanced pizzas, accompanied by wizened roots, unfolded before me. Once more I was very near to tears. Then it struck me as odd that food was clearly so much more important than sex in my shaping of this atrocious northern world. Well, it would be too cold to take your clothes off, ever. A montage of erotic scenarios therefore faded away with fife and drum into the distance. I tried thinking hard about the money. And for a while, this worked.

I had a shower and then sat dripping on my friends' post-modern rug, while I pulled every single filthy garment out of my travelling bag. The only thing left that was crushed but clean was my interview suit. I had worn that for a terrible thirty-five minutes, then run straight back from the chamber of confrontations to the Bed and Breakfast where I was a refugee on the third floor. The suit was scrunched into the bottom of the bag and I re-emerged, booted and spurred, ready for flight.

I peered dubiously at my smart high heels, the fraudulent woman's complete disguise, and decided against them. There I stood, thirty-eight minutes later, in lush dark green, ironed white shirt, Wyatt Earp tie, tiny gold studs and Doc Martens, laced up my calves, with steel discs on the toes and heels, in case I needed to rupture someone's spleen. I looked back into the mirror and saw myself, impeccable, extraordinary, Brylcreemed, murderous.

"Go forth and conquer," I leered at my reflection.

The phone rang. It was one of the friends who owned the flat. "F-E-L-I-C-I-T-A-T-I-O-N-S!" she shrieked.

"*Tu parles!*" I laughed, very pleased, and danced a two-step with the phone in my arms.

My boots always give me confidence. I thudded aggressively down the Metro steps and took up two seats' worth of space on the train to Montparnasse. I crossed my legs pulling my full skirts wide around me. I was a great ship on her maiden voyage, my bows still sticky with champagne. I was a 757 touching 40,000 feet. I was a catamaran, winning the Fastnet. I was travelling again. Without the suit or the boots my shoulder bag was much lighter and so I bounded up the escalators into the huge, glass-frosted dome of Montparnasse. I was turning the corner on the last flight when I heard the music.

It was the "Blue Danube" waltz, played by full string orchestra with woodwind and percussion, a mass of wonderful, echoing, cascading strings. I reached the top stair and stopped, amazed. For there in the centre of the great concourse, traversed by rushing crowds, surreal and magnificent, flanked by the computer-assisted ticket-dispensing machines, was an orchestra, a perfect orchestra, glamorous in evening dress, creating around them, stucco, pink cupids, chandeliers, bare-breasted women in great masses of taffeta, shining parquet floors, and the shiver of diamonds. Someone pushed past me. I gazed open-mouthed at the phenomenon. There was no conductor, for they were a dance orchestra and followed the first violin.

As the waltz hurtled towards its triumphant close I heard the roar of applause, rushing out of the girders, cracking the glass, splitting the concrete at my feet. I cried Bravo, Bravo, possessed by uncanny joy. The orchestra rose, turned towards me, an eerie mass of black and white, and bowed. As they seated themselves once more I was certain that the leader nodded and winked. They began the "Emperor Waltz." I held my breath.

All around the life of the great station continued. There was someone buying squeezed oranges, ignoring the cellos, a man grappling with the ticket dispenser, which had swallowed his credit card, a group of schoolchildren jostling each other's slogan-covered sacks. The vast red panels high above us, announcing the arrivals and departures continued to click, glitter and change. In the distance, above the tidal surge of the dancing waltz I heard the hiss of the TGV on the *grandes lignes*. Nothing ceased, paused or changed. Everything was touched by the music. The whole world had begun to dance. Then I noticed that someone was standing beside me.

Who is the other who stands beside you? Sometimes, when you look directly, there is no one there. You are simply aware of a mass, a breath, a presence. I was aware of someone in white tie and tails. But I decided not to look. This was probably a colleague collecting money for the orchestra. Yet no importunate top hat appeared before me. What do you want? What are you waiting to hear? Puzzled, I turned to look directly at the apparition who was now clearly expecting to be acknowledged. Who is the other who stands beside you? Uncanny, familiar, disconcerting, beloved and unknown. I looked into a face I had never seen before and had seen every day through all the years. The slick hair, smooth olive skin, the tilt of the chin, the grey eyes; this was the face in the mirror, glimpsed in the night, the face waiting by the open door, the face in which I knew every line of the smile, the face I had never seen. We knew one another. We had never met.

"May I have the pleasure of the dance?"

I had heard the voice a thousand times. I had never heard that voice before. Who is the other who stands beside you? Who is the angel who waits for your greeting? Who is the other who asks you to dance? I put down my bag and held out my arms in a huge open gesture of liberating joy.

Dancing touches the pulse in the veins, in the lips, in the heart, breaks down dams, explodes bombs, rocks dictatorships into catastrophe. Dancing ends wars, heals wounds and sets the captives free. Dancing lights the stones, the trees, the stars with flame, fills the glasses with wine, breaks the pearls from the chain. Dancing fires the churches and the courts, smashes bank doors apart, scatters the sands in the deserts, melts the polar flows. Philosophy is best done dancing. Without dancing, dancing, dancing, no revolution will ever be complete. Dancing is making love. Dancing contains the force of that great green wind, which will be the destruction and the salvation of the world. So take your partner in your arms and dance.

I heard the steel discs on my boots crashing against the floor. All around me the commuting crowds waltzed into eternity, clasped in one another's arms. I caught my train with only seconds to spare. The great red eyes of the electric brain were alight. The footplates were ready to fold quietly back into the body of the long silver creature which was waiting, waiting to dance away down the lines.

See where the angel waits, elegant, loving, fastidious – with outstretched arms.

The Arrival Matters

For Miranda

The child is bored. I can see she's bored. So far nobody her age has arrived on the beach. We are early. It is barely nine o'clock. The sands are naked, perfect and clean; the sea carefully advancing, retreating, like a dance, one step forward, one step back, a fastidious, tideless blue. I settle my old bones into a wicker chair under a palm tree on the edge of the café's spidery ranks to watch her. She has not yet accumulated the hideous paraphernalia of seaside holidays which she always purchases at enormous expense. She is reduced to a mask, a snorkel, a pair of flippers, which I am holding, and a long coil of pink plastic beads, which she has tied up in uneven loops round her neck like Louise Brooks in cabaret performance. I imagine fatal scenarios in which the beads catch in underwater wrecks, become entangled in the rudders of passing speedboats or attached to the scooping sails of the windsurfers. There goes Miranda, swept away before my eyes like a mackerel in a drag net, and myself heaving and screaming powerlessly under a palm tree, too weak to intervene.

"My dear," I shout over the parapet, "why don't you give me those plastic beads? I could keep them in my pocket."

She looks up resentfully from the sandy pool she is inspecting, embarrassed by my voice.

"I like wearing them," she says, turning back to the pool.

Behind me, five feet below the promenade, the traffic trawls between the lights. No one else is sitting at the tables. The chairs stand rigid on parade, facing one another, the cushions in undisturbed mutual salute. There is no wind. Uncanny and sudden, the waiter appears beside me.

"*Un café.*"

"*Et pour mademoiselle?*"

We had been his first customers from the hotel. She had eaten two croissants and a bread roll, then demanded cornflakes.

"Miranda!" I lean over the parapet and turn my hands into a loud hailer. "What do you want to drink?"

"That green stuff I had yesterday. Which you sweetened. I can't remember what you call it."

I look at the waiter. "*Diabolo menthe, s'il vous plaît. Et du sucre.*"

The djinn vanishes.

Miranda has put on her mask and snorkel and is staring into the pool. I watch her carefully, marvelling at the long brown back and at how much she has grown. She used to have one long thick plait and presented me with a screaming session whenever I brushed it out. We cut it last year into a thick short bob with fringe, ending just below the ear. Very smart, very *jeune fille*. She went off to school looking magnificent, dark blue blazer with badge and Latin motto, *Semper fidelis*, light blue shirt, dark blue tie and woolly pullover, pleated navy skirt to just below the knee – "I hate it, it's too long" – white socks and black lace-ups, lacrosse stick attached to the shoulder-bag – " . . . so that you don't go on wielding it like a Kalashnikov. The police will pick you off and then it's no good my saying that it wasn't loaded, is it?" – there she goes, anxious to meet her friends, get rid of me. Here is Mrs Davies, taking the register on Waterloo Station, Platform Six. "Why haven't you got a ticket, Miranda?" – "My guardian's just gone to get me one. But I signed up for the school train end of last term. Just not soon enough to be on the ticket. I must be on the list." Yes, of course she's on the list. And here I am handing the ticket graciously to Mrs Davies, who staples it carefully on to the huge white expanse of the school ticket. She's found her friend, that dark girl, Mags, and they're already plotting battle plans. You need a battle plan for the autumn term. Decide about the new girls, which one to talk to, which one to persecute – " . . . can we have our lockers back to back in the dormitory like last year? I've got two rabbits. They're called Tinker and Thumper. And a rat. Rats are lovely, don't squirm. I've got a black rat called Lucy. My guardian says we can breed from her. Wait till you see her. You'll want one. Oh, are you going? 'Bye." – One kiss. Dismissed. Adults are an embarrassment. Especially strange-looking old ones with added jowls. But Miranda quite likes having an extensive supporting cast, glamorous parents abroad, three little sisters like miniature mandarins, wealthy sinister guardian with large London house. I come back with her Sony Walkman.

"You'll need this if you've packed your tapes."

The gratitude gets lost in the struggle for a window seat. I nod to the other irrelevant parents, wave once and leave her to it, chattering at full speed to Mags and getting out one of her catalogues to plan the next round of conspicuous consumption. She gets more junk mail than I do. None of it goes in the bin. But there aren't any prices attached to the glossy pictures, just a shabby sheet of A4 slid in the back with huge sums in tiny figures. I stare at it, clutching my credit cards.

She can have anything she wants. Within reason. But what desires are ever reasonable?

I look over the parapet. There she is, up to her ankles in the rhythm of lascivious waves, lick, splash, suck, toes sinking into the sand. There are more people here now. I peer down the beach. Those two children look about her age. But she won't make the first move. They'll have to. Ah, she's chosen her spot in the damp sand and has begun to build. Good idea. That'll draw them. Ramparts first. A moat. Good, I adore a moat. With a sluice linking up to the waves. Blocked off during construction. First set of towers added to the ramparts.

"Do you want your *diabolo menthe* down there?"

No, she'll come up. Knock it off quickly so that no one touches the ramparts. Other two children cautious, watching, but taking no risks, sorting out their sun-hats and beach wear. She's thundering back down the steps, leaving me covered in a light sprinkling of white sand. How do eleven-year-olds, not overtly large, always cause the furniture to vibrate? A cactus trembling on the balustrade. She's back down there again rummaging in damp sand. A windsurfer near her, young man in a wet suit, putting it all together. What patience! What madness! It's taken him an hour to get the thing upright and disentangled. Miranda ignores him. He is very careful not to encroach upon her territory. Ah. The younger of the two children with the pink, topless mother is making a move. She has arrived at the ramparts to parley. Miranda looks up, down, gets on with it as if she has noticed nothing. An awkward, ankle-rubbing, foot-shuffling pause. No concessions. The other child squats and makes her offer. These smooth white stones to decorate your towers. Miranda hesitates. But she is no longer bored.

All right.

The other child is serious and delighted. With her face set like the leader of an orchestra who has just received the conductor's signal, she begins to play. One stone after another carefully embedded in the damp, dark sand. Miranda takes over. No, not like that. Like this. Put them sticking out. To repel the enemy, the spikes and stakes of defence. Now they are both inside the ramparts, building. The second child approaches. Waits to address the commander. Miranda was born to command.

Peer to the right of the parapet to begin my reassurance

operation on Mrs Pink Skin, Pink Breasts, Pink Nipples, Two Children. When children fraternize the parents check each other out. Yes, she's put on her dark glasses, is looking around. Wave, nod, smile, that's the ticket. Ah, she's identified me. Oh God. She's coming up.

The pink woman puts on the top half of her bikini and a long loose shirt, collects her purse and her hat, steadies herself on her feet, sandals hanging over one shoulder, and begins to negotiate the deep sand. She pauses by the castle. All three children unite against her and stare accusations. A word to Miranda who is clearly the eldest. "What?" I can see Miranda wrinkling her nose, squinting. The woman must have spoken French. Ah yes, that's my girl. She's changed languages. Miranda's French is excellent. Should be, after all these trips and those private lessons. Then what language is she talking with the children? All children learn to *parler enfant*. At birth it seems. Here comes the pink mother, negotiating the steps.

"*Bonjour.*"

"*Bonjour, madame.*" Tap the chair for her, make her feel welcome. She's not worried, but puzzled. I always make allowances for the strangeness of my appearance. It's the length of my hair that's unexpected. Unusual it seems, for very old people to have long white hair and to wear it loose. The magician once told me that I looked like an extra on the set for Polanski's *Macbeth*. Funny, I said, I never imagine the witches as fat. Patting my jowls to annoy him. She is smiling, offering me a drink. I am not alarmingly peculiar after all. Why not? *Merci, un café.* She shouts to the children. Three Oranginas coming up. Below us, Miranda has welded the group into a fighting unit. The sea is the enemy. They are facing the sea.

Madame and I are talking sunburn and the need for hats. She describes Miranda as my granddaughter. That'll do. Never contradict their assumptions. People usually come out with what makes them feel happiest. I nod encouragingly, trying to look benevolent and frail. I can always pretend that I haven't heard. She compliments my French. Have I lived in France? Oh yes, on and off. You have to pass through France to get anywhere. I confess to a life in the theatre. She has worked in couture. Her husband is Monsieur le Directeur of Crédit Agricole in this city. He spotted her on the catwalk, ex-mannequin, turned *modéliste*. Oh no, she is going to tell me her life story. I settle down in my wicker chair, darken my glasses by peering into the sun, hand out the Oranginas to a gaggle of sandy faces and listen to the usual woman's story of great expectations, horrific disappointment and unsatisfactory compromise.

Murmur at the correct moments. That's all that's required. She has decided that I am strange, but *sympa*. The English have such leeway in their eccentricities. Being English is like travelling in a ready-made disguise. I am often successfully English, keeping the other identities for rare occasions.

The pink lady rustles in the wind. We sit in companionable silence, watching over our children playing on the beach, while she reflects upon her own narrative. *Vous êtes à l'hôtel? On se revoit? Sûrement. Bon appétit*! She summons the unwilling children. Miranda lets them go. They have her permission to depart. *A demain*? No promises. *Peut-être*. She takes her time making friends, Miranda. If she wasn't given to such terrible tempers she would be an extraordinarily gifted politician. No hurry. No secrets. Her expression impassive. But she can never conceal her anger, or her excitement, and I don't believe that she has ever told a lie in her life.

"You hungry?"

"Mmmmm." Wild nods.

"Were the children nice?"

Indifferently. "Yes, OK."

"What were their names?"

"Josette and Delphine. Delphine's my age."

Leave it at that.

We gather ourselves into baskets. My knees creak as I straighten up and lurch down towards the crossing. All the umbrellas are up now. The café is full. Working people mostly, not tourists. We decide to eat at the hotel. Miranda leans on the button. *Appuyer, pas enfoncer, ma belle*. Curb your tendency to destroy.

The hotel dining-room extends on to the terrace under a canopy of flowering bougainvillaea: purples, oranges, pinks. Beautiful, thick old roots, twisting out of the square slab of earth. I put on my reading glasses to enjoy the roots. Miranda is saying that everything on the menu is inedible. *Steak frites*, ice-cream, pasta. You eat pasta, don't you? There's a *Menu Enfant* with three choices. Under the desserts. Yes, you can have a dessert *à la carte*. Not too much chocolate. Oh, all right. We're on holiday. Me? I'm having *julienne à la crème*. Do you want an Appeltizer? They can get it from the bar.

" . . . *et un porto pour moi. Merci*."

I pause to listen to the colours. Only in the very early morning can I hear the incredible blue. Midday and we are engulfed by that great white light of the south, an explosion of glare, cacti rampant in a huge stone box, the shadows hard and sharp, with the sea wind now rustling the flowers above me. I gaze at the blocks of brightness, remove my glasses, then transform them into abstract shapes, each solid mass filling the circle of space around me. The colours soften and dance, each edge shimmering, loving, so much tenderness and gravity. Colours are serious, anarchic, they lean towards me in huge sensuous gusts.

" . . . you aren't listening."

"No, my dear. I'm sorry. I wasn't. I was talking to my colours."

"Do they answer back?"

"Of course they do. What's the point of talking to them if they don't?"

"Get them to talk to me."

"Not at table."

"Awwwwhhhh. You got them to talk to *you*." Sulk.

"Oh, all right. Listen to the purple bougainvillaea."

Cymbals, trumpets, and big drum over the top. Miranda's eyes are dancing with delight and surprise. She wriggles and the Badoit wobbles on the table.

"Now the pink. The pink!"

Violins.

My avocado arrives, bristling with shrimps. The colours fall silent. Miranda is disappointed, but triumphant.

"You only do things like that on holiday," she says. And puts her fingers in the sauce.

By the time I am drinking my coffee, off guard, relaxed, really on holiday, the terrace has emptied out. Miranda is gnawing at the After Eight box, yawning, and the birds have begun to arrive for the crumbs. The sparrows, glossy and sparkling, chatter and nip. I gaze at them complacently, catching their attention. The waiters have gone. No one is observing us. I sit, harmless and old, disturbing no one. The sparrow asks me to move my feet; a spattering of bread bits are under my shoe. She pounces, eyeing me curiously. I tell her to come on to the table, that Miranda won't hurt her. She hesitates, mistrustful.

"Miranda. Don't move. And the sparrows will come on the table." She stares, pleased.

One, two, three, four of them rapidly descending onto the food-spattered tablecloth. A burst of temper on the part of the first little sparrow, who, incredibly, comes to me for arbitration. On to my hand, babbling.

"Shhh, shhh, shhh," I say to her aloud. "Calm down and I'll shake out my napkin." An energetic, dancing scrabble follows. Miranda is desperate to touch one.

"Don't move and she'll land on your shoulder."

Miranda sits tense as a stuffed Pharaoh. The sparrow, bribed, lands on her shoulder and peers into her ear for a moment, then flutters rapidly back on to my hand, demanding more. The others clear up the table, chattering, scrapping like Messerschmitts. I break my last crust of bread into crumbs.

She hoovers them up with the rapidity of a professional vacuum cleaner.

"That's it, chaps."

One of the waiters has returned. He is watching, fascinated. We are the last people left on the terrace. Miranda claps the sparrows as they whirl and dart among the bougainvillaea blossoms.

"How tame they are," I say to the waiter. He agrees. Waiters are paid to agree.

"Siesta, Miranda. And then your Latin lesson."

She makes the most terrible faces. Discipline must be maintained, old girl. I promise a poem about sparrows.

> *Passer, deliciae meae puellae*
> *quocum ludere, quem in sinu tenere . . .*

And we both cheer up. As we climb the staircase she asks me, "How do you know so many languages?"

"You're always asking that and you never listen to the answer. Languages are only a way of interpreting the world. And during my apprenticeship we were taught to see the world in many different ways. Besides, I'm old and I've been looking at the world for a long time. Far too long, it seems."

"How old are you?"

"Oh, very, very old. Old as the hills."

"I always ask you that and you never tell me the real answer. Never really truly."

And she's right.

She hangs over the bannisters and looks at the perfect oval beneath. The hotel is also very old, an eighteenth-century building, refurbished with antique furniture, giant arrangements of flowers on polished mahogany tables at every landing. I pause, listening to the aphids muttering in the roses. The whole world speaks. More languages than human beings ever hear. You're getting away with murder so far, my dear. English, French and Latin. Three Western languages. Full of poetry, however. Which will teach you to listen to the poetry of the wind in dry grass, the damp hum of the rising tempest in the pine trees, the calling owls in the night, the waves singing to the rocks, the long notes of the whales at a hundred fathoms. But English schoolgirls at expensive private schools begin with French and Latin. Well, that's a start.

Our suite of rooms has two linked balconies, bright with azaleas in vast Roman pots. Shared bathroom in between our bedrooms and a separate boudoir for my boxes. Red cushions on the white wrought-iron balcony chairs and a vast red awning with bulbous, vulgar tassels, which Miranda uses as punch bags. She has discovered that the awning is electronic-ally controlled by a gadget which looks like a television remote control. For the first twenty minutes she sat on the balcony making the awning perform a series of curtseys like the figures on her musical box. I let her do it. Better than having her push all the buttons to summon the djinns. She stretches and yawns as we enter our darkened rooms. The awning is down, the windows are open, the shutters closed. We hear the clink of crockery on the terrace below. The white light batters the shutters, long cracks of glare, horizontal, against the fresh, cool gloom. We are facing south. The warm wind from North Africa stirs the hanging sheaves of white lace. This is the wind which the birds ride on their way home. Miranda kicks off her sandals in the bathroom. I wring out her bathing costume in fresh water. By the time I look in she is asleep, nose in the pillow, cheek already turning pink with sunburn. By tomorrow she will have turned into my Ariel, a wily, stringy, golden djinn. Never very easy to make her wear any-thing. But tomorrow she must wear that hat with the green eyeshade. Or else.

I totter back to my own room and fold up on the edge of the bed. Now that I am old my body seems heavier to carry from place to place. I get tired, my knees ache, my back curves sadly like a broken tree as the vertebrae melt together, a breaking string of beads. I am old, I am old. It was high time to summon my magician. I have done the right thing. I lie down with a grunt, closing my eyes, retreating into the vast green void, through the doorways of perception, the great gates of the mind.

For a moment the room sways liquid before me: large inlaid cupboards painted with cupids, borders winking back mother-of-pearl, the long lines of white light, the lamp, hooded with cream silk, a gilt mirror, dark above the marble. The mirror melts gently into green and then I see the avenue of trees, pruned straight as ballerinas; an avenue of poplars, a geometric line stretching out into a stately, infinite green. This is my kingdom, my island. I may go where I please.

I see a house far away. What kind of house? A large seventeenth-century house with a terrace in front, old baked tiles and large pots overflowing with aggressive geraniums. Bright white light pours onto the gardens and I shade my eyes, stare at the open French windows and the lace curtains stirring in the draught. Ah, her old house. So that's where I am.

Memory and desire are playing games with me again. How many times have I longed to see her since? I adjust my collar and tie, straighten the white summer jacket, find myself no longer corpulent, but energetic and deft, a heavily built eighty-five kilos, magnificent at forty, thick short hair, greying but mightily distinguished, slicked back, mounting the steps like a lion in season. Where is she? Laughing. You always heard her laughing from a long, long way away. Laughing in the kitchens, in the bathroom, in the vegetable gardens, in her woodlands, laughing at the day's bright shadows, Fatima's new parasol, the cook's failed sauce, the new little chickens, bantams, balls of fluff, *mignons comme tout*, laughing into the telephone, at a silly film, at someone else's sexy pseudonym in the Minitel Rose. Look at that, dear – SUPERMAN, *BRUN*, *MINCE*, COOL *MAIS SYMPA*. Probably a young macho thug with spots and halitosis. And she taps in her own messages, laughing, laughing. What pseudonyms do you use? I ask, annoyed that she has not commented upon my suit, my nails, my rings, my perfumes. Oh, she laughs. I use all my names: La Luna, Artemis, Diana, Chandra, Cynthia. I promise to be erotic, changeable, passionate, never bourgeoise or practical. I promise to embody their dreams, fulfil all their desires, make love in every position. I have the most amusing replies. My Minitel post box is full every day.

They will all be wickedly disappointed. I am having a tantrum of jealousy.

My darling lion – she kisses her greetings, sweeping my jealousy aside – that tie, it's atrocious. Jowly people should never wear bow ties. It makes you look as if you're developing a goitre.

I haven't got jowls. Indignantly.

No, but you will have. I shall never see them, thank goodness. Wild laughter. However, I shall crouch inside them. When you caress your jowls you will be caressing me. She turns off the Minitel with a snap. Stands back measuring my performance critically. I take a few strides across the carpet, turn, frown, strike an attitude. She applauds my gestures, bounds forward, adjusts my cuffs. The mother-of-pearl cuff links must show; part of the effect, part of my mystery. Fatima, Fatima, she shouts. Come and see. It's quite wonderful.

And Fatima materializes out of the breeze, rustling the curtains. Well, well, she says. What a transformation. Fatima is Moroccan; a djinn eight feet high, all golden bangles and elegance. She is of Berber origin, dark-skinned and broad-browed with wild scented hair. I won't kiss you, sweetheart. I'm covered in John Innes 2 and Vilmorin slug poisons. She peels off her gardening gloves. Cynthia is ordering tea and lemon biscuits to celebrate my arrival.

Afterwards we walk in the gardens. Fatima takes my arm and shows me all the improvements: rockeries, lily ponds seething with goldfish, a trout stream, an aviary filled with exotic birds, new landscaped orchards with cherry trees, damp mossy lawns on the edge of the woodlands, hollyhocks and foxgloves, a virgin forest of vegetation, apparently under control. Costs me a fortune in irrigation, says Cynthia. But I won't use the stream. The farmers think I'm mad. Our water's metered. Two dry seasons running and I'll have to make paper notes myself to fill up the deficits in our accounts. You've no idea what Fatima's gardens cost.

We walk across rough meadows with dandelions and mole hills, bordered by acres of young, rising sunflowers. Hideous when they turn black and dead, says Fatima. She kept one field green last year, Cynthia comments, and the farmers were so puzzled that they couldn't let it be. They seem to have lost all their respect for the miracles of nature. They called in the government inspectors from the Ministry. I had a sudden moment of panic when I saw them taking soil samples and turned it black overnight, so that it looked like all the rest. And the result of that was a special committee of investigation, a television programme, a bevy of experts, further digging for soil samples, tests on the water table and the local *gendarmerie* interviewing us both. They even wanted to inspect Fatima's *carte de séjour*. Fatima is laughing. You wouldn't believe it. Monsieur le Maire himself came round to apologize. Of course we said we knew nothing, saw nothing, never heard of anyone tampering with sunflowers. And since then we've been much more careful.

I look across open country, down the lines of green poplars, at the cows browsing in the summer heat, the brisk, varnished gates which Cynthia paints with her own hands. I dream of living here.

It will all be yours one day.

She has read my thoughts.

I would rather live here with you.

Not possible, darling. Fatima's voice.

A pause.

"Listen," says Cynthia aloud, "what you can't have, inherit. You are our inheritor."

That night we are sitting by the windows looking out into

darkness, gorged on spiced lamb, couscous, Fatima's vegetables, red wine from the Midi, full of the sun, warm from the mistral. There are fireflies glowing among the bushes. I can hear the stream pouring across the silence. Cynthia speaks.

We are ambassadors. Think of your task in these terms. Usually we must remain invisible, discreet. We are the people no one else suspects. We must be above suspicion. Eccentricity is useful. All other strangeness can be put down to our harmless peculiarities. We intervene, but we never interfere. We never share our secrets. We never explain ourselves. We are no different from the others, yet we are absolutely separate. We see different things, different patterns, different worlds. In some ways our time is parallel to theirs, but our centuries move at a different pace. They hear rumours about us, gossip, myths, fairy tales. Mostly, they fear us. The human race is very fearful. Like animals on unknown ground. They fear difference, strangeness, the ones who are other than themselves. We take up our places, as men, as women. We remain in disguise. Over thousands of years we have shown them our visions, our powers, our extraordinary hopes. Sometimes they listen. Their imaginations transform us into priests, or into gods. But sometimes they will regard us as monsters, as demons. They will seek our lives.

You must be always on your guard against them. Make friends with them, yes, of course, you must know them like the back of your hand. We live alongside them in a stifling intimacy. You should know what they will think, what they will do, seconds before they do themselves. Calculate, predict, deflect. You can never love them. You must find your lovers only amongst ourselves. They are a people to be managed, but they are never to be trusted. You must negotiate the world carefully. Choose even your enemies. Continue your work quietly. Be silent, unobtrusive. We will ensure that you have resources enough before you become our inheritor.

Yes, I know that some of us choose the path of open confrontation. That is a very risky business. I have tried it myself. We are sometimes impatient with their stupidity. If you do act openly, make sure that you have enough money to buy yourself out or to escape. Their colossal vindictiveness seems to recognize no limits. Remember my warnings. I am quite serious. Sometimes we have been powerless to help each other. And that has caused me great grief in past years. When those I have loved have been lost. The shape of our lives may be different from theirs, but we are mortals too. I will not allow you to be destroyed. Neither you, nor Fatima nor the magician. Nor the child who will be your inheritor. I will watch over you always. You have my word.

We sit silent, serious, uneasy and oppressed. With the air of an impresario who is introducing the last act – a comedy – Cynthia rises.

"And now," her laughter is tickling her throat, "on with the dance. Your education, my dear, is complete." She bends down and kisses my forthcoming jowls. "What will you have by way of *digestif*? Cognac, Armagnac, Benedictine, *crème de framboises*, Calvados or just a little Glenfiddich?"

Fatima stands on the terrace in the warm night teaching the fireflies to dance in figures of eight like mad sparklers. They bounce on her fingertips, settle in her hair, pick her out in fairy lights, form roses of moving light on the toes of her shoes, leap over her breasts and her belly like a waterfall. She becomes a mass of lights. But there is Fatima's gleaming enigmatic smile, illuminating the darkness.

And I awoke in darkness, aware of Cynthia calling, calling, years later, the darkness surrounding me and the woman calling. Where are you? Where are you? No answer, only the darkness echoing. I took time off from my business affairs, telephoned Miranda's school, leaving a sequence of phone numbers, addresses and fax machine contacts, bought open tickets on foreign airliners, packed my bag – what clothes to take? Hot, surely? When did Cynthia ever choose to live in a cold climate? I sit on the edge of my bed in my tall London house, listening, waiting.

It is Fatima's voice that I hear. Orchids, my darling. I had always wanted to grow orchids. Come and see my collection.

I take a plane to the jungles of South America.

There are twelve of us, all assuming crash positions at touchdown, hoping that, like the Apostles, we are a lucky number. I can see the smoke from the pilot's cigar, that he doesn't inhale for the thirty seconds before landing. Wild cackles on the wireless. Do we have clearance? Nobody knows. Glimpsed through the yellowing oval, green, roofs of green, sandbags, broken-down buildings full of bullet holes, a machine gun pointing at the sky, twenty hefty bumps and here we are, jolting towards an enormous red and white sign. DRINK COCA-COLA.

We all cheer. We've made it. The pilot turns, gushing clouds of smoke; he has gold teeth, with dirty epaulettes on either side of his smile.

No such thing as customs, but we are all searched anyway. I bribe the young man going through my pockets with a Casio solar-powered calculator. We part friends. There is no information desk, no taxi service, no town, no hotel, no telephone that works. There is a mini-bar selling ancient bottles of Orangina and Seven-Up at staggering prices. They haven't had any Coca-Cola for years. I poison myself with a mouthful of cold chemicals and beg help with transport and information. The single-storey barrack building empties out. My fellow passengers vanish, consumed by the jungle. I am left alone with one silent black boy and the mini-bar.

I am looking for Miss Cynthia Harrison and her companion, Miss Fatima al-Sabbah. Who live somewhere here in the jungle.

"Orchids," he sighs dreamily, "you should just see Fatima's orchids."

Hours later I am still bouncing on a green ripped plastic seat, a .303 Lee-Enfield wedged against my thighs, the driver toothlessly singing as we heave through the overgrown joke of a road in an old US army Jeep. The vines scrape the roof and the bush tugs against the doors of the vehicle. We rise and fall in water-filled potholes, the engine competing against the barrage of noise outside in the saturated, breathing jungle. Huge, leering colours peer into the Jeep, breathe green in a thousand shades, mutter, scream, vanish. I sit mute, assaulted on all sides by uninvited sensations. Cynthia's laughter rings out, coming closer every moment.

We enter a twilight green gloom of damp and strange cries. Stop to remove part of a tree, fallen in front of our wheels. This takes two hours, our only weapons a rusty saw and an axe. How do they manage to live here? I climb back into the Jeep, sweating and stained with red bark. I have not spoken, but the driver replies.

"They know the jungle, those two. They take precautions. They are friends with all the jumblies, googlis, afreets and animals. They even patch up the terrorists. Fatima says she's above politics. Cynthia won't have anyone bleeding on her doorstep. But you should just see Fatima's orchids."

I stare at him amazed. Then, our knees banging against the green tin dashboard, we jolt dramatically into a large sunny clearing, a meadow of whispering knife-like grasses, and far away, on a little rise, shimmering eerily like Gawain's castle, is a colonial-style residence, all verandahs and balconies. Hibiscus and poinsettias lean over the white marble steps. Huge painted butterflies perch on the open shutters. There are no defences, no gates, no sandbags, no barriers, no electric fences, just a large handsome house, confidently there, shining slate roof of imported materials, wooden walls, lattices, mosquito screens, cream, grey and green, everything gleaming with certainty. A water-filter system and a series of ponds to the left with a shiny green mesh covering them. Some kind of solar-powered device on the other side, metallic panels on raised structures like football stands, a large shed for the generator. They must be self-sufficient. Clustering at the back of the house, a row of giant greenhouses. And yes, I can see them now: a military barrage of poised colours, penile stamens, huge opening lotus blooms, lush curving slit leaves, carved like cacti. Orchids, Fatima's orchids, magnificent, sinister, matchless, perfidious, extraordinary. I climb out of the stationary Jeep to do some more incredulous staring. I am Stanley, presumptuous, unbelieving, just arrived.

The driver grins. He is waiting for a large, promised pay-off in dollars. I mumble my thanks and fill his hands with green notes. Nothing stirs in the house. The Jeep bangs noisily away in reverse, then plunges back into the all-engulfing green. I approach the house cautiously.

Then Fatima steps out of a slight damp wind that raises my collar like a dog's hackles and appears on the steps. She is unchanged; straight, startling, impressive, her hands cool, her rings shining. She waits for me, unsmiling.

"Don't be afraid." This is all she says.

The interiors are darkened, cool, smelling of wild thyme and lavender. We pass across uneven, polished boards into a room full of stillness. I stumble against old brocade sofas, antique tables with priceless Japanese vases two feet high covered in rampant dragons. Nothing fits. Disoriented, I reach out for Fatima. She takes my hand; she is cool and smooth as a lizard.

"Don't be afraid," she says again.

A small movement in the corner of the room and a figure sits up on a pale blue sofa. It is still Cynthia, but I would never have known her. She is now terribly shrunken, extraordinarily aged, her hands transparent, her back curved into a widow's hump, her skull almost bald, only a faint coating of white hair left. Her eyes are the only living things left to greet me. It is as if her spirit has already begun the longest voyage. She is aching to depart. I hear her whisper. "At last. At last."

I take her hands, feel the veins, the bones, frail as a quail's claws. "It has been very hard waiting for you." The death's head cracks into a hideous smile, pale gums, many teeth gone. "But then, I was always impatient."

Fatima rustles in the doorway. She gives me a glass of pure cold water. Cynthia whispers urgently. "Stay now. Wait. It may be hours yet. Don't leave me for a moment. When I am dead go out of the house at once. You will have to walk back, even if it is night. You won't get lost. Fatima will be your guide. Follow her. Whatever form she takes. And don't look back."

She subsides, gasping, on the cushions, too light now to make any impression on the blue silk surfaces. I sit silent beside her. The light never changes around us. Her breathing is so faint that I have to stare at the slight rise and fall of her blue dress to make certain that she still lives. Every hour or so Fatima returns with another glass of cool water. Exhausted from travelling and sleeplessness, I watch beside her late into the afternoon. I lose track of time. Then I hear the birds gathering. Violent blues, greens, yellows, orange, red; brilliant parrots and humming birds, glossy macaws, dull brown monsters with faded lemon beaks and weird cries; they gather on the balconies and window sills. I see them rustling against the mesh. Fatima comes again, with another glass of cold, pure water. But this time, in her other hand, she carries an armful of giant purple flowers, succulent, spangled with white, torrid with scent. These she places in Cynthia's hands, folded across her shrivelled, diminishing body. I had thought that the woman was no longer present to this world; but she speaks, very quietly. "Thank you, my dear. These are the first flowers for me. And the best."

Then her vanishing begins.

The babble of the birds suddenly increases, then ceases altogether. In the silence that follows I feel rather than hear the change in her breathing. My own body is quite cold, despite the heat. Cynthia begins to ebb, like a retreating tide. Her body collapses, like that of a vampire at the coming day. Inside the light blue gown she shrivels and cracks. The light fades, suddenly, rapidly. I catch my breath, reach out to touch her. She is dropping away from me into the dense, tropical void that will swallow her. She is running water, stealing over a precipice. I cry out in terror, Cynthia, Cynthia. I clasp her dwindling claws, which are still clutching the orchids. As I touch her she becomes dust. The dress is empty. Only a light spangled cloud drifts among the gleaming blooms, across the cushions. The birds batter at the mesh, then vanish into the coming night. I have spilt the water on the table, it drips into my shoes. The house reels, empty.

Fatima. Calling urgently. Follow me, follow me. I stagger out, tripping on rugs, out on to the grey steps of the verandah. The jungle looms, grey-green, whispering. Before me is an outline of glittering fireflies, it's too early to see them, they wait for nightfall, they are dancing in patterns. It is Fatima. Follow me, follow me. I stumble across the clearing, haunted, terrified. Can this be the road? I have abandoned my suitcase. My face and hands are bleeding, my mouth dry with fear. I forget Cynthia's warning. I look back.

There in outline stands the ruined house, overwhelmed by lichen and creepers; the glass in the greenhouses is smashed and jagged, the ponds bubbling with green corruption, the empty door swinging in the night wind. Follow me, follow me, chant the fireflies in desperation. I plunge after them.

On the return flight the pilot tells me what a lucky escape I have had. That zone was controlled by the terrorists who, had I been seen, would have shot me at once, no questions asked. Two women? Living alone in the middle of the jungle? Unheard of. They would be murdered in a matter of weeks. A pitiless place, the forests of his country. He had wondered at my reasons for coming here. The English are mad; his teeth gleam. Enterprising, but quite mad.

" . . . Follow me," Miranda is delivering a lecture in my left ear.

"What's that, my dear?"

"You were snoring. Ughhh. Huge snores. Like a horse."

"You can poke me if I snore."

"Did. You didn't stop."

"I'm sorry. It's the wine."

She grins.

"Where are you going?"

"To try out the hotel pool. I've already had a look. Just two people swimming. It doesn't say special hours for children. Can I go down?"

The hotel pool. I run the contours of the chlorinated water through my mind. Blue tiles, yellow parasols, someone rubbing cream onto her knees, a pergola laden with flowers, lemon trees, tubs. Ah! there he is, all brown skin and muscles, sitting with a towel round his neck – the lifeguard.

"Yes of course, my dear. I'll follow you down."

She rushes out, goggles and snorkel hanging over her shoulder like a gas mask. I sit up, my head aching. Four o'clock. I reach for the telephone. Hesitate. Am I being paranoid? She's nearly twelve. Swims like a fish. Cynthia promised. Yes, I'm being paranoid. So what? I ring down to the lifeguard.

"Hello. It's Sven, isn't it? Yes, we're staying at the hotel. My ward should appear in a minute. She's eleven, blonde, wearing a red T-shirt and black and white striped shorts, carrying a mask and snorkel. She can swim perfectly well and will no doubt dive straight in at the deep end. Usually does. You'll keep an eye on her? Thanks. I'll be down in half an hour."

Funny that they never wonder how we know their names. No one has ever asked me how I knew their name. People like being recognized. As if they were film stars. Maybe we're all busy starring in our own films. Well, Cynthia, it's my turn. And the fourth act. I won't let you down by being cowardly or hesitating. Still, I wish you were here to encourage me. All my life, whenever there was a problem, I went to Cynthia. *Non sum ego qui fueram: mutat via longa puellas.* Mustn't forget that Latin lesson. Where's my clean shirt? Ah, pink. I look awful in pink. To be old, fat, jowly and grey is to be able to wear bright pink shirts with impunity. Long live liberty. It's not that you suddenly look good in a colour that doesn't suit you. It is that you have ceased to care. That's what I loved you for, Cynthia. You had the gift of setting me free. And you didn't give a damn about other people's opinions. Other people's love was an elaborate sequence of games and traps. A sort of endless labyrinth of intrigue. A dishonesty of Homeric dimensions. My own included. That has to be admitted. But you, you, all fire, elegance and certainty. You had the gift of telling truth, saying no. You always said no to me. And God knows, I asked. I begged. Fatima's ironic smile. Nothing pleases the god of love more than bitter tears. How can you still long for what you have never had? One woman's smile, one woman's touch, the scent of her in the night, meetings in cafés, journeys together, knowing when the phone rings that it will be her. Her voice, above all her laughter; the laughter I can still hear when I hold my breath. Well, it is my destiny that I could never love another woman, nor cease from loving her. *Cynthia prima fuit, Cynthia finis erit.* Mustn't forget that Latin lesson. Rise. Accept your destiny. Get out of bed.

She loved the Côte d'Azur. The con-men, the fashion shows all down the Promenade des Anglais, the restaurant terraces, the frauds, the gangsters. *Le milieu*, she called it. Knew them all. Personally. Even knew who'd done it, when some doctor who ran a private clinic in Marseilles was found shot dead at the wheel of his Mercedes. I thought she ought to testify. Fatima told me not to be ridiculous. That was the summer they rented a villa in the hills above Cannes. There were fourteen doors onto the verandah. I counted them. The walls were pink stucco and the shutters an incredible, luminous blue. I used to sit in my bedroom doorway humming to the colours. They got dressed up and went out on the town, night after night, Cynthia gleaming with gold, low-cut shining dresses and never a trace of the sun on her shoulders. Remember Fatima's terrifying Chanel angles, all *haute couture*, individually designed, expensive and glamorous. Would I lend them my car? And eat anything left in the fridge? God knows where they went. They came back, sometimes at dawn, exhausted, ruffled, singing, two birds of paradise on one colossal spree. It was during that summer, years and years ago, on the Côte d'Azur, before it became a glorified chip shop and campsite run by the Germans, that I first met the magician.

The evening unfolds in my mind. I see Cynthia, littered with jewels, uncoiling like a serpent. Her back white against the great blue dome of the evening sky. I hear her voice. "Well . . . would you like to hear a genius playing with a second-rate orchestra?"

Fatima drives along the coast road to Nice. I sit beside her clutching our hats. Cynthia in the back like a millionaire. The roof is folded up in a staircase of shining brackets and white leather. And we all have our knees near our chins. The smell of the sea, still fresh, gentle against the warm rocks, wild thyme on the rocky hillsides, the earth, the crags, red, red, ferocious in the evening sun. And then we arrive at this hotel. Yes, it was different then. A sea-going palm court of walnut tables and art-deco chandeliers. The dining-room linen, starched and ironed, so much so that we used to wrestle with our serviettes which were folded into crowns on the tables before us. Real silver cutlery, and thick, heavy crystal. All the waiters wore white gloves. I wonder if they've put it all away in boxes awaiting some forthcoming era when extremely wealthy people confine themselves to stealing from the poor and give up stealing plates. There were lemon trees in the foyer then. Cynthia poured her gin over the roots of one of them when no one was looking and hung her lemon slice on a branch. It wasn't there in the morning so somebody must have actually polished the lemon trees. We dressed for dinner then. We still do, but not evening dress. There was a ballroom. I think they now call that the leisure centre. I looked in, to find that the polished floors were still there, but that it was filled with gymnastic apparatus, heart attack preventatives, and an aerobics class. Well, I danced here too. Once. And on Sunday evenings there were concerts.

Cynthia was being terribly serious. "Listen," she said as we took our seats, "I'll introduce you afterwards. He won't find it amusing. But you will."

This was the kind of audience who rustled their programmes and waved to their friends. This was the kind of orchestra that had been playing background music for years. And the magician was the kind of soloist for whom each performance was like the last judgement. I never saw him come on. I was listening to Fatima. The leader of the orchestra was already there, mopping his temples with his handkerchief. There was a murmur, then a hush, then a burst of clapping. I put on my spectacles and looked.

He was very tall and thin as a pencil. Black hair, slicked back, parted at the side, razored at the back, then very much the fashion. A strange, lined, cold face, all twitches and tics. No lines of a smile. Stiff plain shirt, plain white tie and tails. I stare at his hands. He wears no rings. He sits still for nearly a minute at the piano, mastering his nervous jerks, and I see his face again. It is in the process of changing, becoming colder, utterly silent, uninhabited, the north slope of a bare mountain. The audience quietens, becomes quite still, waiting.

I can't for the life of me remember what he played. I can only remember the urgency and the edge, the drama of his arpeggios; and my mounting conviction that the man could not be quite human. Sitting there beside the only woman I have ever loved, I fell in love again.

With a magician.

There was an outrageous assault of clapping at the end. We howled our bravos, trampled our programmes underfoot. We would not let him go. He introduced his encore.

"This is a traditional piece from my country." A nerve in his cheek jumped like an anxious cat. On the edge of my seat, I held my breath while he spoke. The accent was that of some unspecified Central European state, now crumbling towards capitalism. The music was a burst of insolent desperation, like a gypsy dance. It was also, subtly, full of anger and demand. We exploded in a roar of eulogy.

In the bar afterwards Cynthia kept her eye on the door. We sat drinking impossible cocktails and I found that the palms of my hands were wet. But I never saw him come in. Suddenly, there he was, a foot away from me, kissing the tips of Cynthia's fingers and looking at her suspiciously. Then I saw what I had been too far from the small stage to see; amid the eerie, nervous movements of his face, his steady wolf-grey eyes. Cynthia was doing her duty as the hostess. We were being introduced. I held out my hand, which he ignored.

"*Enchanté*," he snapped, with a military click of the heels.

"Will you have a drink?" Fatima suggested.

"Yes. Thank you. A glass of water."

"We very much enjoyed your performance."

"Thank you. But I play for myself. And I was not satisfied."

"But it was quite marvellous."

He grimaced impatiently.

"Do you have many forthcoming engagements?"

"Yes."

"Oh. I expect that you play in all the big cities."

"Yes, I do."

We were all trying hard. Cynthia had become a pillar of charm.

"I'm told that you are engaged in New York . . ."

"Yes. Next March. For a month. Seven concerts."

"It must be a very lonely life. Always travelling . . ."

"I do not find it so."

"Do you have a family, perhaps . . . ?"

"No."

He was becoming more and more abrupt. Cynthia is never

rude. Curiously, neither was the magician. He listened to her questions with terrible attention and became alarmingly monosyllabic. He never volunteered any information of any kind. She attempted to enlarge the discussion, to move on to general topics. We seconded her, but he defeated us at every turn. His face tensed, and his hands, clutching one tall glass of bubbling mineral water, trembled slightly. How did he ever touch the piano with such steady certainty? I smoked cigarettes, staring intently at this strange, wonderful face. Fatima finally extracted one tiny personal detail.

"What on earth do you do to relax?" she asked smiling. I could see that she was fascinated by this extraordinary visible mass of insecurity.

His gaze, all ferocity and honesty, rested upon her for a moment. "I make magic," he said.

"Magic?" Cynthia crowed. "Then you are a real magician?"

"Yes," he said simply.

After an hour of bemused discomfort on all sides, he began to take his leave. He had never addressed me personally during all this time, but now, bowing to each of us in turn, he extracted a small white card from his inner pocket. As he opened his jacket I caught a glimpse of scarlet silk. The card, like a joker's trick, was handed to me. And so were the words, a pair of folded gloves.

"This is my address. I would be grateful if you would come to see me. Whenever is convenient."

Another bow. He is gone.

Cynthia is jubilant.

"Fatima! Did you see that? And in front of us both? Well, my dear, that takes the biscuit. A *billet doux* and an assignation. In public. All done in public. What style!"

I peered at the card. It was my turn to dissolve into facial tics and shaking.

We always remember when it was that we first saw the person we love. We relive those moments. Try to recapture every tiny, irrelevant detail. What you wore, who was with you, your glance, your eyes, your hands, the scent of your hair, how you turned towards me. We vie with each other for precedence. Who was first in love, who was first stung by desire, who made the first move, decisively and unmistakably, who first had the courage to act. Now I try to settle you in my mind, to make you real and comfortable there. It is a matter of hours before I see you again. Irresistibly, descending the staircase in the heat of this late afternoon in early summer I look in on the silent bar, now utterly redecorated, refurbished, rearranged. Nothing remains of that night forty years ago. I lean heavily against the wall. I am old, grey-haired, bloated and frail. And I see you, not as you were then, but as you are now, still tall, wolf-like, predatory, glancing to left and right, still a cauldron of nerves before you perform, the gaunt timeless figure of a famous man. You are the real magician. I see you coming towards me.

Half close my eyes. You are there, you are gone. I hold you in my mind for a second more. Then let you go.

There are jolly shouts from the swimming-pool.

"Watch me dive. Look, look. Are you looking?"

Yes. I'm looking.

Splash.

She surfaces, hair slicked flat, sleek, pink porpoise. Gasp, gulp, splash. Breathless, clutching the bar at the edge of the pool.

"Did my knees bend? Sven says I've got to keep my knees straighter. And my ankles together. They bent a little bit, didn't they? Look, look. I'll do it better this time."

Greatly relieved, I slump down under one of the yellow sunshades to watch Miranda's performance. Sven bows slightly, then gives commands, arrogant as a duke. No. More spring. Bend the knees. Then straighten. Aaaaaarch your back, Miranda. That's it. Splash. Ungainliness suddenly becoming grace.

She shakes herself off like a dog.

"I've forgotten my towel."

Sven lends her his. He's obviously good with children. He promises her another lesson tomorrow.

"Latin verbs," I say menacingly.

"You promised a poem. Spoilsport."

I assure her that we will have the poem as well as the verbs. We sit translating Catullus in our half-darkened rooms. *Passer deliciae meae puellae . . .* The poem she chooses to translate unseen proves to be highly unsuitable. I cast an eye down the uncensored text and flinch. I suggest that she need only go as far as line six. Miranda smells a rat immediately and with the unnerving acuteness of childhood asks what these words mean. No, these particular words. They're verbs, aren't they? Evasion is hopeless. I confess to a torrent of obscenities which sends her scurrying to the dictionary. Luckily, she cannot yet grasp what is involved in the perversions described. Catullus's rage is translated with fascinated care, but remains dark to her. Saved by innocence, O Furius and Aurelius, yet menaced by fellatio and sodomy forevermore.

Then we decide to go for a walk in the cool of the day. She darts off to get her baseball cap with the green shade and, no doubt, a mass of other equipment which I will end up carrying. But she is enjoying herself and so am I. We negotiate the traffic hand in hand and set off down the *rue piétonne*. The city is pink and gold in the evening sun, blinds still down, shutters half-closed. Dogs off the leash trot past with amiable certainty. We pause before chic clean shops, whose prices are breathtaking. I stand peering at dresses which signal instant elegance and bankruptcy. Only a woman with a figure like a pair of tongs could wear that. Wouldn't suit me. Go for solidity and tweeds, Cynthia advised. Pale colours in linen for the summer. Try to avoid looking like a chicken brick. Should I bury my jowls in scarves? No, never be ashamed of magnificence, whatever form it takes.

Miranda has bounced to a dead halt in front of a patisserie

window. Swimming begets desperate hunger. We gaze in upon the chrome plates presenting fruit tarts, *millefeuille, bavarois*, macaroons, florentines with nuts affixed, *mousse Grand Marnier, religieuses*, éclairs coated with chocolate or coffee cream, laid out in a gently chilled context, like dead soldiers waiting to be identified. "Can I have . . .?" Miranda begins. Yes, yes, but not before dinner.

"But I'm hungry now."

But you won't eat . . .

"I shall die of hunger."

You're not starving.

Sulk.

"You never let me have any chocolate."

Out loud. "What a lie, Miranda. I've ruined your teeth singlehanded."

"Oh, pleeease."

All right. Give in.

We enter the grotto of silver and shining gold. Every surface – metal, glass, tile – unsmudged. Great vats of coloured sweets like an alchemist's elements, arranged in parade on the shelves. Belgian chocolates with white ladies' faces in deep silver vats, liqueurs in red and silver paper, slabs of nougat peppered with nuts; a rich, fresh perfume, mysterious as memory, engulfs the shelves. A young woman, used to tourists, nods and smiles.

Miranda takes a long time choosing. We come out with several éclairs, a bag of mixed chocolates and a *cerises, ananas* and kiwi fruit tart. As we wander down the cobbled streets lined with flowering tubs, through the old town, I eat all the fruit tart and she starts in on the chocolates. The season is just getting underway. We watch the beach equipment stores checking their new stock. New trainers and T-shirts arranged in patterns on the pavement like a modern art exhibition. Germans, older people mostly, a few Dutch. That's all. The French school holidays haven't yet begun. We wander into a square flanked with palm trees, ornamental flower beds, a green-wire-fenced playground and a sand pit, settle ourselves on a bench and champ away at the éclairs. The sun is still violently hot on our knees despite the hour; there is a sprinkler whirling on the off-limits square of lawn. Miranda notices the players before I do.

"Look," she says, "there's going to be a show."

Three young men are busy erecting the tall striped stage for a puppet play. It is like a little free-standing pavilion, decorated with pointed, flashing lights. Other children have gathered to watch. Miranda keeps her distance and a firm hand on her bag of chocolates. Back she comes.

Séance 18H. pour les enfants du quartier
10 francs par personne

"Can I watch?"

I go with her and we sit down on the benches in the evening light watching the boys rummage and mutter in a mass of boxes and ropes. The preparations are as potentially fascinating as the performance. I remember a Yeats play I once saw with the magician, which was prefaced by a quite extraordinary ritual called the folding and unfolding of the cloth. The magician explained that it was intended to increase the audience's concentration. We all fell silent, mystified. In fact, the folding and unfolding of the cloth was easily the most intelligible aspect of the play. I said so. And the magician was furious. He liked Yeats.

One of the young men comes out of the little tent beside the stage wearing a bowler hat and braces. He has a big red and white loudhailer, a clown's nose and a little bell. The *quartier* is being summoned to the performance. Off he goes round the neighbouring streets with a comet's tail of children running after him.

By six-fifteen we are nearly fifty; rustling, giggling, eating, hitting each other. Miranda wolfs the last of the chocolates. A dog circles the pavilion, barking and barking. The bowler-hatted boy has taken our money and is now adjusting his accordion. Music. Action. The curtains jerk back to reveal a Christian knight confronting a Saracen. Incendiary material. I look round. Half the children are Beurs, of Arab origin. They don't seem to care. Confrontation. Battle. Victory. These are the grand emotions. The stuff of epic, opera, the great films. The red cross knight and the Saracen have the same fierce painted faces and shiny bucket helmets. Handy dandy. Who is the justice and who is the thief? We will never know. I eat one of the éclairs. There is a good deal of singing and fighting and hitting one another on the head. I am Sir Bryan Ting Ling. I am Sir Bryan Rat Tat. I am Sir Bryan as bold as a lion. Take that and that and that. We are thoroughly enjoying ourselves.

After this racially offensive dust-up, the young men turn their attention to sexual politics and a domestic scene between the French equivalents of Punch and Judy. Punch is wearing a blue beret and has the same large red nose. Miranda recognizes him. But now the battle is not equal. Judy loses her grip on her rolling-pin and wails pitifully as Punch hits her on the head with a pair of scissors. All the children roar with laughter. He is going to cut her tongue out because she has nagged him. Suddenly, Miranda loses her temper.

"It's not fair," she mutters fiercely, "it's not fair. Judy hasn't got her rolling-pin."

Punch has got hold of her long, red velvet tongue. He really is going to cut it off. Miranda pokes me desperately.

"Do something."

The audience is delightedly divided. Should he do it? Shouldn't he? He asks the children. You should never ask the children. Sexists, sadists and savages, down to the three-year-olds.

"*Oui, oui, oui,*" they all roar.

Miranda has a British sense of justice. She supports the underdog every time.

"It's not fair," she hisses. "Do it. Save her."

Normally, we never interfere. We intervene. For the hell

of it I break the rules and the scissors. Suddenly animated with a will of her own, Judy snatches up the other half of the severed blade, whirls it in the air like Excalibur. Yells that Punch should now defend himself. The children are thrilled with this new twist. Some of them are standing on the benches, yelling at the tops of their voices. One of the young men is so startled I can see his hand creeping down the puppet's strings to check if Judy is still attached. She is. But his creature has taken a rebellious turn. She whacks god's thumb with the scissors and he hastily withdraws.

The show must go on. Punch and Judy fight it out on an equal basis using the scissors as broadswords. Neither wins. They fall exhausted over the kitchen table. The boys hastily draw the curtains to rapturous applause.

Miranda is delighted. She hugs my arm.

"I knew you could fix it."

I have perfected her evening. Chocolate, then justice. Miranda has a sweet tooth and a streak of unfailing integrity, a little weakness and a great strength. We sit in a glow of self-gratification. She is pleased with me and I am very pleased with her. Mustn't leave the loose ends untied. When the three young men take a bow, I suggest to them that it was their idea that the scissors should fall asunder, that it will be a wonderful new development in their act. That they should play it that way, tomorrow and tomorrow and tomorrow. They are asking for more money. I give them fifty francs and slink guiltily away to catch up with Miranda, who is hunting for a Pizzeria.

Yes. Let's eat out. Pizza.

She chooses cheese and tomato. I end up peering at a raw egg looking up like an eye from a circular arrangement of pepperoni and anchovies, exact as a French garden. We are sitting in a Pink Pizza Palace, which has the same fake 1930s decor and Jazz Age music as the one in Paris, in London, in New York. Well, children choose the familiar.

"Do you want another Coke?"

"No thanks."

"Miranda. Did Cynthia and Fatima often talk to you about the magician?"

"Yes. Lots. He's not a magician really. He's a pianist. I cut out those pictures of him and you from that French magazine. Cynthia and Fatima said that he used to dance with you."

I drop my fork. Scandalized.

"They said what?"

But she's not really interested. She's thinking about something else.

"Danced. You danced tangos in the ballroom of some hotel."

I become somewhat indignant.

"It was in the ballroom of the hotel where we're staying. Forty years ago. And the place was a lot more expensive and exclusive than it is now."

"Oh. Was it?"

"And we only danced the tango once."

Forty years ago might as well be the Middle Ages. My life before she was born has only ever been of marginal interest. Children are like very wise Buddhist monks and only live in the present.

"Why just once?" she asks mildly.

I am so perturbed that I decide to smoke a cigar. We walk out into the warm night. Miranda is yawning a little. She decides she will watch a video in bed, seeing that I've paid for it. *Merlin L'Enchanteur*, in French.

"Would you like to meet the real magician?"

"Is he coming?"

We stroll through the lighted streets, hearing voices, music, the sound of people eating behind shutters left ajar, a television thriller in which the entire cast is engaged in shooting each other dead.

"Yes," I say, as if I am talking to myself, "he's coming."

For the first time Miranda really listens.

"When's he coming? Here?"

"Yes. We'll meet him at the station. Ten o'clock tomorrow morning. He's staying at our hotel."

Doubtfully. "Shall I like him?"

"Did Cynthia and Fatima think you would?"

"Oh, yes. They said I'd adore him. They said they did."

"Then take their word."

We have reached the front. A light sea wind kisses our faces and we hear the low thud of the surf on the beach, smell the sea. For a moment I am no longer old and fat and frail. I have all the force of maturity, the energy of youth. And my lover is coming.

But it is not so easy in the early morning of the following day when the mirror tells me that I am very very old and that the only reason Miranda does not think me hideous is because she is used to my warts, my wrinkles, my flabby hanging jowls, my hooded eyes, my thinning hooked white brows, my long white hair. I tie it all back in a pony-tail, a parody of the way the young men wear them now. This makes me look not only ugly and old, but mad. I lay out all my tailor-made expensive clothes, linen, pale colours, silk cravats, fresh shirts, white-starched or soft cotton, my summer jacket. Nothing will make any difference. Old age is not shameful, but it is hard to make interesting. Settle for being tidy and clean, if you can no longer be glamorous. I decide to choose plain, discreet elegance. To be wealthy if you look closely, and to smother myself in perfumes. I shall patrol the station reeking of orchids. I shall carry a walnut walking stick, engraved with a name and a date on the ivory handle. That is my concession to sentiment. I shall choose a very thin gold chain. The mirror replies that the final effect is magnificent, but bizarre. That I look eerie, well-heeled, unchanging, strange, and very, very old.

"Miranda. It's nine o'clock." I open the shutters and lower

the electronic awning with the vulgar tassels. It hums and whirrs. She doesn't move.

"Miranda. We're meeting the magician at the station and I've ordered a taxi for half past."

She groans.

"Miranda. I've been up since seven and I'm on my nineteenth nervous breakdown."

She opens one eye. Then both. Wider.

"You're dressed up for a party. Or a wedding. I don't have to get dressed up, do I?"

"You have to put something on. Shorts and a T-shirt will do. Brush your teeth. I can't go alone."

"Why not?" A rebellion is brewing. "Why can't you go alone?" More insistently this time.

I decide to be honest. "Because I'm scared shitless. Come on. Give me some moral support. I don't ask often."

Miranda sits up in bed and looks at her toes. "OK," she says.

We roar away to the railway station in a taxi driven by a servant of Satan. He too is all jowls and has a murderous countenance. Miranda is eating a *tartine*. He tells her not to drop crumbs in his taxi. She looks wounded, then goes on eating, leaning out the window. I sit biting my nails.

The station is all sunshine and hollow echoes, an airy vault traversed by birds. It is spotlessly clean. One of the tramps addresses me in English. I give him ten francs and ask him if he is in fact British. No, he replies, but we all speak English nowadays. Especially the tramps in Antibes. *C'est nécessaire maintenant dans le métier. Tout à fait.* We stand in front of a vast pale grey board, animated by a computer. We have ten minutes to wait. The TGV from Paris *arrivera* ... *pas de retard*. Oh God. I'd counted on a few more minutes. I'd hoped he would be late. The child is bored. I can see she's bored. She's pressing all the buttons on the sweet machine, just in case there's a Kit-Kat jammed in the system. What's she got? Five francs. Triumph. Ah, Miranda, that's enterprise. He is coming. I can see the TGV, well past Toulon, Cannes, coming, coming, battering into the tunnels, sleek in June sunlight, long silver and blue carriages, leaning on the rails like a roller-coaster, coming, coming. Yes, of course you can keep the five francs. Finders keepers beneath a certain sum. No, don't use it on that machine. It didn't work last time, did it? Go and get a Kit-Kat at the kiosk. Yes, I'm OK. I'm nervous, that's all. I haven't seen him for five years. Where in God's name are all these dogs going? That's the second one I've seen trotting past, collar and name tag attached, but no owner in sight. I can't bear it. This is the end of the line. He has to get off. The train goes on to Genoa? But he wouldn't make a mistake, would he? I've summoned him, dammit. I'm not senile yet.

"Do I look all right, Miranda?"

She holds my hand, chewing a Kit-Kat that is melting messily over the other hand.

"Don't worry. You look great." She grins, quite at ease. Odd, it's usually Miranda who gets into a stew. Especially when we're meeting her parents and her three little sisters, who all seem to be called Matilda. We are surrounded by other inhabitants of purgatory. All waiting. Peering down the empty line for the deep-set red eyes of the TGV. One lady is holding a bouquet of tulips. Yellow and red. Tulips. Funny, tulips aren't in season. Must be forced in an Icelandic greenhouse. A symphony of sixes and threes. Have you looked?

"Six petals. Six stamens. That's symmetry."

The announcer blathers unintelligibly. There can be no mistake. This is the train. He is coming.

Then we see the creature snaking round the corner, slowing on the turn, the huge moving hiss. Miranda stands on tiptoes, suddenly excited. "I won't know him. Is he still like those pictures? What does he look like?"

"Very tall. Straight short grey hair. No, he'll be wearing a hat. He always wears a hat."

The doors are opening in computerized slow motion, the

little steps unfold and descend and they pour off, all tired, carrying plastic bags, briefcases, canvas overnight cases, coats, magazines, umbrellas, all the detritus of travelling. Miranda leans forward, peering at the mass of unknown faces. I can scarcely see, for anxiety and tears.

And in fact I don't see him first. Miranda does.

"Isn't that the magician?"

I follow her gaze.

He is there, a long way off, coming up the platform. Yes, he is wearing a hat. A large black hat which shadows his face. But I can see the line of his jaw clearly, as if I could already touch it with my finger, the slope of his shoulders, even in this heat he is wearing a warm coat, taller by a head than the man next to him, carrying one small bag, as if he had packed and left in a hurry. A vigorous older man, very straight, very tall, very thin. This is the man Miranda sees.

But I see the past. I see his face close to mine. I see the steadiness of his features in repose. I hear his voice, the accent always surprisingly marked, asking me a question, pointing something out. He is a man who is always tense in public, or in company. To see the moment in which he shrugs off the famous pianist, the nightmare of interviewers anxious for the personal angle, and becomes himself, warm, intimate, funny. I am the sole witness to that contentment and trust. It is a strange thing to watch someone you have loved as if they were alien, a stranger, yet to remember insane, irrelevant details: his hatred of coffee, his allergies, his hands cutting bread, the smell of his body in the mornings. I stare into the past. The magician looks up.

Then flat panic overtakes me. I snatch Miranda's hand, turn and run. Amazed, she keeps up. We rush out of the station, hurtle down the street, plunge into the nearest café. People stare. One of the passing dogs actually starts barking at our heels. I expect to hear the Dickensian shout of "Stop Thief" at any moment. We collapse on slashed plastic sheeting. All my well-controlled rolls of fat are shaking. The entire population of the bar, five old men and *la patronne*, turn to stare. I put on my dark glasses. Miranda gazes at me as if I were finally certifiable.

"Aren't we meeting him after all?" she asks in a stage whisper. The bar waits, incredulous, for the next development.

"No," I hiss back. "I can't. I'm not ready."

"Why not?" Irritation backs up amazement.

"Because he'll guess why he's here. If he doesn't know already."

"But I thought you'd invited him."

"I have. Sort of."

Miranda gives up on the interrogation and becomes practical. "While we're planning what to do next, can I have an Orangina? And then can we go to the beach? If we aren't going to confront him before lunch. I promised Josette and Delphine and they're bringing some stuff for me to try out."

Madame arrives, lips pursed. I look too rich and too weird for this bar. The video machines thump and mutter to themselves, scoring own goals, staging car crashes and eliminating opposition.

"*Un Orangina. Et un café. Merci.*" I turn to Miranda. "What stuff?"

"A raft we can blow up to use on the water."

"Can they both swim?"

"Dunno. I suppose so."

She stares out of the window, on the watch, just in case the magician walks past. I have definitely lost all credibility. Complete defeat in the very first round. But it is all terror and excitement. Miranda enters into the spirit of the thing.

"You ought to have your back to the door. Just in case. I'll keep a lookout."

"Yes, do. I'll be all right in a minute."

"Have some cognac. You usually do when you're shaky."

"Not at ten in the morning."

"I think the coast's clear." She scampers back from the door. "He must have taken a taxi."

I'm calm enough now to search for him and she's right. He did take a taxi. Ours. With fresh breadcrumbs all over the back seat.

The second line of attack or defence, we now don't know which is more appropriate, is lunch. I decide to fight round two in the dining-room. We have two hours to kill and Miranda insists on the beach. I have no fear of encountering the magician. He will go straight to his darkened room and sleep till midday. We march back to the hotel at a brisk pace.

"It's a shame that you're going to take it all off again," says Miranda regretfully. "You really do look great."

"I'll be too hot. Anyway, sod it. He'd probably have been so horrified to see me that he wouldn't have noticed."

"Why should he be horrified?"

My trousers are XXL and yet they still feel tight over my thighs. "Well . . . not exactly horrified. But unpleasantly surprised."

"Don't you ring him up?"

"Yes, I do. From time to time. But we had agreed not to see each other for a while."

"Why?"

"Oh . . . that's all very complicated. Listen. Do you want your snorkel today? You might. I'll carry it. And take a hat. You're not going out without a hat."

So off we go to the beach. As we reach the lookout post of the beach café, Josette and Delphine, already faithful admirers, set up a triumphal screaming. Miranda, Miranda. She is very pleased and roars off to greet her public. Mrs Pink Breasts waves to me and puts her all into supervising the inflation of the sea-going Lilo. I sit up on the terrace, resplendent as royalty, tremendously excited, counting off the minutes, letting my coffee go cold. Miranda has forgotten all about the magician. The raft has become her magic island, where each child has a turn at being Prospero. I notice that

Miranda's turn is rather longer than those of the others. Ariel and Caliban froth and surface in the breakers, one of them is wearing her mask and snorkel. They exist only to do her bidding; but she exists only to command. I smoke another cigarette, reflecting on the fact that I have always existed outside the universal law of the ruler and the ruled. I cannot complain. I hear Miranda's piercing French. Let's sail further out, offshore, she cries. Mrs Pink Breasts and I leap to our feet, our maternal warning systems whirling like flashing ambulances. No, Miranda, no further. Ah well, perhaps we are all controlled by higher powers.

By the time we are installed in the hotel dining-room, sandy and a little flecked by dust, seated in front of an array of impeccable white linen and silver cutlery – "It is all hall-marked, I checked," says Miranda, "and I thought you said that this hotel is less expensive than it used to be" – we are in a whispering dither of excitement. Will he come down? He must. We are hiding behind the brown leather menus and silver tassels, pretending to choose, when he surprises us both by coming in from the terrace, a glorious gust of sunlight behind him. He is hatless, distant and tired. I see the tiredness in the hunch of his shoulders, the way in which he massages the back of his neck, an old nervous concert tic, a habit of years back. He sits down in the window on the far side of the dining-room.

"He's here," Miranda whispers theatrically.

"I know."

"What are you going to do?"

"Eat lunch. But watch. I've prepared a little *coup de théâtre*."

Sure enough, as the magician fingers his squeezed orange juice, the most restrained of apéritifs, the *maître d'hôtel* enters with a bouquet of a dozen white roses. There is a moment's hesitation while he consults with the waiter. No. There can be no mistake. He has signed into the hotel and this is the famous pianist himself. And these roses are surely from a lover of music, a passionate admirer. Holding the bouquet at a little distance as if it was an explosion, the black-coated, white-gloved old man, my unwitting ambassador, advances across the room, bearing down on the unsuspecting magician. At first he is very taken aback, bows in discreet acknowledgement that he is indeed who they say he is, then quietly glances round the room. Miranda and I plunge inside our menus. When I look at him again he still has his back to us. But I know him too well. Every nerve is alive with tension and alarm. He has understood the signal. A dozen white roses.

"*Steak frites,*" says Miranda, "well done, with ketchup."

By twelve-thirty the dining-room is surprisingly full. A large group of business executives on a marketing seminar install themselves between us and the magician. Miranda can just see him from time to time.

"Eating an omelette. No wine," she reports after a long stare. "He hasn't once looked at us." Disappointment. We are undercover agents, longing to be found out.

"Did you put a note in the roses?" she asks hopefully, "saying which table we were at?"

"My dear, there are forty people in this dining-room. If he wants to see us all he has to do is stand up and look around. He'll acknowledge us when he's ready. Not before."

We are eating profiteroles when I begin to notice the whispering. The magician has been recognized. The rumour has spread. On holiday? A concert? I've got three compact discs of his – one with the Berlin Philharmonic and Herbert von Karajan conducting. *C'est pas vrai. Il est plus maigre que dans les photos. Il habite Paris. Mais oui, c'est lui . . .* The whispering follows the magician now, wherever he goes.

Suddenly he gets up, finishes his Badoit while standing, and, without looking round, goes out of the *porte-fenêtre*, on to the terrace. The noise in the dining-room increases as we all begin to speculate out loud.

"Gone," cries Miranda. "Are you going to follow him?"

"Not yet."

I decide to smoke a cigarette. Miranda wrinkles her nose. "It's bad for you."

"I'm sorry, dear. I'm overwrought."

"Well, smoke the other way then. I hate it."

The *maître d'hôtel* approaches with a folded note. "*Il y a un message pour vous.*"

Miranda cannot wait. She climbs halfway up my shoulder to read it. And there is his writing, firm and clear, in English.

> *I had already guessed you were here. Please*
> *don't send me any more roses. I shall wait*
> *for you on the terrace.*

"Do I come too?" demands Miranda. I reflect for a moment, no longer anxious.

"No. Not at once. Go and see Sven for a bit. But you can't go into the pool until two-thirty. At least. After all that ice cream."

She protests. "I always get left out when things are exciting."

"Since when are adults talking about the past exciting?"

"But Fatima and Cynthia said I'd love him. Why can't I meet him?"

"You can. But not yet. Go and see Sven for a while. He's there. And he's bored. Then come and join us and I'll introduce you."

Miranda sets her lip for a moment, then ingeniously, wonderfully, disobeys the spirit of my command while keeping to the letter. Off she goes across the dining-room, out the terrace door, and no doubt as close to the magician as she dares, to get a really good look. I finish my cigarette in amusement, then creak to my feet at last.

He is sitting under the bougainvillaea, where we sat yesterday, in my place, looking out at the sea, as I did. Then he reflects upon the floating lemon in his tea. I go straight up to him and kiss him on both cheeks. He is exactly the same; older, but firm, straight, cool, grey-eyed. The lines around his mouth are perhaps a little deeper, the nervous tic near his left eye is still there. As we sit silent, close, assessing the changes in each other's faces, we cover a great deal of the ground, the lost years. Finally he speaks. Again, in English.

"All right. Explain what this is all about." I had forgotten the timbre in his voice, the foreignness of his accent, the effort he makes to speak. I promised not to be cowardly, or to hesitate.

"Look at me."

I force him to see me as I am; very old, very frail and very, very tired.

"Now do you know what this is all about?"

He turns quite white with shock and fear. "Why me?"

"Who else?"

"You summoned me then?"

"Yes."

"No . . . no . . ." He is fiddling with the spoon, crushing the lemon slice into the cold tea.

"Listen to me. There is no one else. Only you."

"I can't. I refuse."

"You aren't able to refuse. Don't be such a swine. I went to Cynthia. I travelled across effing jungles in hair-raising planes. All I've asked you to do is take a train to the Riviera."

"That's not all you're asking me to do."

"It's your responsibility. You are my inheritor. Miranda will be yours."

"My God. You mean I've got to take over her guardianship? A bloody British schoolgirl. Have you gone mad? Look, I live alone. I'm very far from retired. I still work. I still travel . . ."

"No. That's in order. It's all foreseen."

"And there are legal complications . . ."

"No there aren't. All the deeds are with my London solicitors. A dossier is waiting for you along with the house keys. In worldly terms you will find that you are my sole inheritor. You now have a huge house in Regent's Park as well as a château in the Corbières. And a great deal more money. Have the decency to be grateful."

"Listen . . . I can't."

"You have no choice."

He is silent for a moment, looking down, his face a mass of terrified tics and jerks. Then he looks up and makes a very unexpected declaration.

"I can't because I still love you."

"Do you?" I am very touched. "I never stopped loving Cynthia. Even when she had the audacity to summon me to the end of the world."

His eyes are upon me, reading me like a score, steady, measured, heartbreaking as he has always been, the same.

"Yes. I still love you. As much as ever."

And then we see the same thing. A long ballroom floor of polished parquet, the balloons snapping. It is carnival. We are all masked and in fancy dress. Cynthia and Fatima are Hollywood Orientals in veils and harem trousers, and we are both wearing Fred Astaire DJs. Music, maestro. And we dance the tango, swooping, bending and gliding to each other's rhythm, with all our lives before us. For the first time the magician smiles. His whole face changes, the anxiety and the tension are gone. The facial tic steadies.

"So you see, my dear," I say, "it is not so very terrible. Don't be alarmed."

I hear Cynthia speaking through me. This too is part of our traditions. No harm will come to you, nor to me. You have my word. I will follow you wherever you go in the world. I will be with you for ever. The magician's hand covers mine on the table. He is laughing, a full, rich ironic laugh.

"So? How long have we got?"

"A day."

"A day? You're a fairy tale. You act it all out like a fairy tale. What on earth can I say? Shall we dance?"

And now we are both laughing. Someone at one of the other tables turns round to watch us. And here is Miranda, who could wait no longer. She had been hoping for a row at least. And here we are laughing. She is very indignant and pinches my arm.

"My dear, don't be aggressive."

"I'm not." Sulk.

"Let me introduce you to the real magician."

He stands up. "*Enchanté de faire votre connaissance*." He bows.

Miranda stares at him. It is the first time in her life that anyone has ever addressed her as "vous". Then she astounds us both.

"*Moi de même*," she says with perfect formality, and shakes hands with the magician.

We all sit down to look at one another. As we do I realize that everyone else is looking at us; through the windows, from the gardens, standing at the terrace door, people are filtering out, filling up the tables. The whispering is increasing. It will develop into photo opportunities and demands for autographs.

"Listen," I lean forwards towards them both and we become three conspirators, "we have to get out of here."

Miranda is thrilled. The story has become one of flight and pursuit.

"Do you have to go up to your room?"

"No," says the magician, feeling his wallet.

"I want to. I have to." Miranda won't say that she has to pee in front of the magician. But he guesses.

"I've got it. The loo by the swimming-pool and we go out the bottom gate."

"It's locked," I object.

He looks at me witheringly. "Since when have we ever been bothered by locked doors?"

"Oh. Can you do things?" Miranda asks him delightedly.

He strikes a pose. "I am a real magician."

Cynthia and Fatima were right. She already adores him.

"Listen," I say, "we split up. You two go out the bottom

gate and wait for me at the beach café. I'll go upstairs to create a diversion. And I'll phone for a car. We'll walk slowly down the promenade des Anglais and Budget can catch up with us. We look sufficiently odd so that she can't miss us."

"Hertz do a better deal," objects the magician.

"*Merde*! Don't question me – one of us works for Budget."

Someone is standing at the magician's elbow. It is an earnest young woman clutching a compact disc of his music. Will he sign the programme notes, under his picture, just there, *désolée de vous déranger*. The magician bows, pale with fury, signs with a flourish, bows again, will not speak. O God. There is a little burst of clapping. Quick. He offers his arm to Miranda as if she were a lady and away they go, under the arching pergolas of bougainvillaea.

I catch up with them at the café. By this time they are hysterical with laughter. They have been to the Beach Boutique and are wearing funny straw hats and multicoloured dark glasses.

"What do you think of our disguises?" asks the magician. His hat has a little band in luminous letters saying KISS ME QUICK. Miranda's slogan says SUGAR MOON.

"You're out of your minds," I sigh, very pleased.

We stroll away down the promenade, Miranda between us, in a nightmare parody of the nuclear family. This strikes Miranda, who has attached herself to us both, an arm on each side, and swings her heels from time to time, dislocating our shoulders. Watch out, here come the Monsters. Then a wild fit of giggles. But nobody stares. It is *de rigueur* on the promenade to look weird.

Our Budget driver is a smart young woman in an orange and white uniform, black stockings and high heels. She kerb-crawls for a moment in the little white Renault 5, peering at our dark glasses.

"Yvonne," says the magician after listening for a moment.

"You're out of practice, sweetheart," I reply, "it's Yvette."

He laughs and waves to her. Amid a barrage of honking and flashing she gets out and kisses us all on both cheeks.

"*Voilà, les clés.*" The magician snatches them up.

"Aren't you going to drive?" Miranda knows that I hate being driven.

"No. The magician says I do it by remote-control and he gets so frightened that he has to take his beta-blockers."

"*Le contrat, l'assurance – tout est dans le dossier,*" Yvette reminds me. "*Bon courage, mes amours – ciao!*" She is gone, dancing across the traffic.

The magician spends a little time fiddling his way up and down the gears. I remind Miranda that safety belts are now the law, even in the back seat. We all adjust our dark glasses like gangsters. And open the windows. The heat smothers our faces. And then we jerk away into the mass of traffic. Miranda leans back, watching the city hum and juggle as we move faster, picking up the motorway feed lanes. We launch ourselves on to the Autoroute de l'Estérel and shoot out into the fast lane. Our registration number ends with O6 and the magician drives with such verve, style and certainty that no one would ever know he was not driving home. In fact, he does know where he's going. And he has shed his funny hat. Miranda is trying it on in the back seat. Now she is wearing both like a church steeple, one on top of the other. She lets my hair out of its elastic band, and then I really do look like a witch. I lay my choppy fingers to my lips. The mountains loom over us. We plunge into a series of tunnels. A large dark drop of water splatters the windscreen. We burst into sunlight, a glitter of sea, white light, chalk cliff, dark again, with a rush of cool air through the car. A bright white oval, waiting 200 metres ahead. And again we are engulfed in a torrid explosion of white light, a moment of resurrection, and then back into the long dark roar. We drive along the level yellow gleam. Miranda and I are tunelessly bellowing out songs from *The Wind in the Willows*. We still have the video at home. I watch it from time to time, even though she's much too old for it now. I am Badger in the Wild Wood. She is Toad of Toad Hall. We both prefer Mole to Rat, and we always loved the songs.

We pass out of the tunnels. MONACO and GENOA appear on the great blue and white panels above us. The magician drops away to the right and we curve at terrible speed round a hairpin bend.

"Up or down?" shouts the magician as we shudder to a halt at the traffic lights.

"Can we go and have tea in Monaco?" Miranda asks wickedly.

"No," the magician and I snap in unison as if we had spent weeks in rehearsal.

"Thought you were rich," says Miranda saucily to the magician. "We're rich."

"Not that rich," I say hastily. He smiles.

"We're not dressed well enough to get out of the car, Miranda. In fact, I don't think that the car is posh enough to stop. And anyway, it's a waste of time. The magician would be recognized and we'd end up having dinner on a yacht with one of his fancy friends."

"Great," she says, "can we do that another time?"

"Up, I take it," says the magician and we begin a hairpin climb up the edge of a precipice, leaning out of the window and gasping at the white banks of rock, the scrubby bush, the first pine trees, apparently rootless, leaning out into mid-air. There are houses perched like birds' nests at every level, cars suspended on non-existent ledges; below, narrow terraces with olive trees. Sometimes there are rock falls, narrowing the road. We drive on, in terror of another car coming the other way. Occasionally we see a letter box at the bottom of a tiny stairway up the precipice, but even when we lean out and peer upwards we cannot see any kind of habitation. Two birds of prey circle one another in the upward draught of hot air from the sea. The heat releases its hold on our throats.

A battered panel covered in gunshot wounds appears on

the right at the head of an even narrower gravel-covered tributary: PEILLE 4,5 KMS.

We surge up the sheer face of the mountain in first gear. Miranda peers over the edge at the giant cacti growing in imaginary soil. The air now smells of wild thyme, fresh wind, the sea. The light caresses rather than assaults the rocks. We can look back down at the road we have already driven, hundreds of dizzying feet below. As we creep round the edge of the headland we see the gleaming white dome of the conservatory, challenged by a crucifix, high above us and still far away; stretching round the bay, the city, gleaming with new high-rise blocks, pushed against the sea by the hills behind.

"Oh, this is brilliant," says Miranda as we arrive in the village. "Are there any other tourists and can I have a cake?"

The village is a curious mixture of dilapidated authenticity and opportunist commerce. There are two German cars and one Dutch pulled up alongside the church. The local *papeterie* sells postcards of the incredible views, the observatory, the golden crucifix and one or two heroic *pompiers* mastering the 1986 fires. There is a *boulangerie*, a souvenir shop and a post office. The streets are too narrow for cars, so we patter down the stepped, cobbled pavements. Miranda is on the lookout for cats, peering at the geraniums, drugged with fertilizer, pouring over their pots. The establishment that has bagged the view and the cliff terrace is a bar/resto/hotel with prices that the magician decides must be actionable. But we go in anyway and establish ourselves at a command post by the telescope under a red and white sunshade.

The magician hands Miranda a two franc piece for the telescope before she has asked. "You'll see better without your dark glasses. No, point it at an object, not the sea – try fiddling the focus."

"What do you want to eat, Miranda? You'll never get through a *millefeuille* after those profiteroles. Shall we share one?"

The magician and I sit looking at the view, at the other tourists and then at each other, while she investigates the view at close quarters.

"I think I can see our hotel. The lower terrace. Not our rooms. They face the other way. Hey! There are ferns in the rocks and I can see this little pool with water coming out of a lion's mouth. Can I choose some postcards?"

"I love this," says the magician, listening to the silence and the wind's breath. "I love being a tourist. Not living here. Having no responsibility."

"Why?"

"Well . . . if there was a revolution in Paris I suppose I'd have to take sides. Join the commune. Man a barricade. Here, I'd just go home. Being abroad's even better. People can be murdered while they're standing next to you. And if it's not your fault, you don't have to make statements. You just get your embassy to fly you out."

"Has it ever happened?"

"Not really. There was a demonstration outside the concert hall in Berlin. I was only in the the first part of the programme. So I was having a drink before listening to the Ninth. I like listening to the choir. Well, I was in the bar. Everyone else had gone inside. And the demonstrators stormed the building. Barman called the cops. The riot police were there with water cannon and tear gas within seconds."

"What did you do?"

"Slunk behind the bar, sat on the floor, kept my head down and finished my drink. Wasn't my quarrel."

"But what was it about?"

"Oh, I dunno. Israeli musicians. Pro-Palestinian demonstrators, I think. You'd have found out all about it, read everybody's leaflet and then made a speech."

"You're right," I smile. "Do you think that's a waste of time?"

"Everything except music is a waste of time. Sometimes I resent my position. Hate who I am. There are days when

I feel trapped within both my identities. My public life and my private mysteries. But here . . ."

He suddenly becomes serious. "Is there any unfinished business you want me to deal with?"

"No." I look at him calmly. "Nothing. Nothing has been left unfinished. You will be Miranda's guardian for the next ten years until she is twenty-one. By which time she will be perfectly capable of deciding her own life for herself. She is already. She takes her time making friends. But she's not a hermit like you are. It will be good for you. Don't take her to too many concerts. Or operas."

He smiles. "You've had an amazing journey. You take my breath away."

"With us it is not only the journey which counts, my dear. For us, the arrival matters."

"I'll see to that," promises the magician gravely.

But here is Miranda. Can she have another two franc piece for the telescope? She doesn't ask me; she asks the magician. I watch her collect the money, smile cautiously – she is not sure of him yet – and then bounce back to the telescope. The two franc piece does not go in willingly. She gives it a thump. Rusty technology yields beneath her mighty hand. She glances round at us guiltily to see if we disapprove. The magician nods. She grins. The process that I have set in motion can no longer be arrested. I gaze out at the unending, unyielding blue, exhausted, but satisfied.

We talk a little about the past.

"The unfinished business is between us then," says the magician morosely. A warm breeze stirs his grey hair like a lover's kiss.

I take my time replying. "Perhaps we could finish the business without picking it over?" I suggest peaceably.

He looks up. "You never used to avoid confrontations."

"My dear. That comment simply tells me that you have decades before you. I have only slightly more than twenty-four hours. Confrontations now seem to me to be perfectly useless. They are, after all, based on the premise that there will be plenty of time to sulk, feel regretful, write outraged notes, slam down phones and send each other dozens of roses."

"Our love affair in a nutshell," he comments gloomily.

" . . . and we both loved doing it or we wouldn't have gone on. Listen, we still love one another after forty years. How many married couples can claim as much? Better still, we have remained friends. And there is nothing unfinished. We both behaved badly from time to time. Unfortunate, but given our characters, quite inevitable. Death makes the odds all even."

I light a cigarette. He wrinkles his nose.

"I wish you wouldn't smoke."

"I won't die of lung cancer between now and tomorrow night, dear."

"But if I've got decades ahead of me I've got time to develop it. Blow all your poisons the other way."

We sit looking at each other with good-natured resentment. Miranda bangs her bum down on the plastic chair and sits swinging her legs. "Are you rowing?" she demands hopefully.

We walk up to the observatory, which turns out to have a military atmosphere. The path is steep and rocky, littered with yellow and purple flowers. The magician helps me over the roughest, most uneven passages. Miranda bounds ahead, screwing up her eyes against the wind, shaking imaginary beetles out of her hair. I can hear her singing. When we get to the top, the view overwhelms us; the huge blue curve of the bay vanishing into an aureole of white light. Boats pepper the uneven blue shades of the Mediterranean, the cars melt into single streams like pencils that bend round the coast. The wind increases to a freshening blast. The magician takes up an impressive pose, one leg balanced against a rock, and throws his head back, like a postcard of Beethoven. Miranda starts clapping. She climbs cheerfully up the railings beyond which there is a sheer and jagged precipice. I begin clucking like a desperate hen.

"Go on," says the magician wickedly, "fling yourself off. See if I care."

"My parents would write to you," she threatens, coming down anyway.

"Your parents! Cynthia would turn up – furious."

"You said she wouldn't be coming back." Miranda looks at me accusingly.

"She said she wouldn't, but I don't count on anything."

I realize that the process of my vanishing has begun. Time becomes fluid. I sit breathless on the peeling bench by the lookout, feeling it creak beneath me. Cynthia, like a thunderstorm sensed in heavy weather, is coming closer and closer. I watch the white rocks speckled with lichen. Breathe the wild smell of gorse, heather, thyme, feel the sweat on my collar, on the side of my face. All my senses are uncannily alert. The stark landscape and the great white light all breathe, speak, becoming animate beneath me. I gaze suspiciously at the cracked concrete slabs under my feet which should stay silent, being man-made. As I peer at the flecked blue and white pebbles, they simmer and rustle in the heat. The magician is suddenly beside me, his arm round my shoulders.

"Are you all right? You've gone very white."

I flick the sweat out of my eyelids. Reassurance is the name of this game. "We have just scaled an Alpine precipice, my dear. At an undignified rate of knots. I'm a little breathless, that's all."

Miranda brings me three flowers. Huge, blue, spiky thistles, with a little blue furze of petals on the crown.

"I pricked my finger getting these for you," she declares, aggrieved.

"Thank you, my dear. These are the first flowers for me. And the best."

I arrange them in my buttonhole, contented at finding even the words waiting for me to occupy their sounds. The rocks and the wind recede a little, hold their breath. I take the magician's hand. It is cool, firm and thin. He looks up into my face, tentative and alarmed.

"Don't be afraid. It has been very hard waiting for you, that's all."

"Will you tell me exactly what to do?"

"No. But you won't get it wrong. You haven't given a bad performance for thirty years. Don't start now."

"Let's slither down this mountain. It's after five o'clock."

"Are there any snakes?" asks Miranda, lifting a vast stone cautiously. "And if I found one, would you make it dance?" She looks up at the magician.

"I'm a professional magician. Not a Hindu snake charmer."

"OK. So what can you do?" She takes his other hand as we hover over each uneven, pebbly step.

"Usual things. Rabbits out of top hats, vanishing scarves, flight of doves, eggs and playing cards out of your ears. Naked ladies packed into coffins and chopped neatly in half."

"Really?" Miranda is impressed. "How do you put them together again? And why isn't there any blood?"

"Professional secret. Mind the prickles."

We teeter slowly down the sheer flight of steps, the observatory's huge white dome receding above us.

"Where was the cross when we were up there?" asks the magician suddenly. "I can see it now but I couldn't when we were there."

"I have no use whatever for the icons of conventional religion," I snap back, a little irritable because one of my prejudices has been remarked.

"But you're very religious," observes Miranda, "you just don't like other people going on about it."

"Perceptive little madam," says the magician.

"Oh? Religious, am I? Well, it's been used as a reason for killing us off in large numbers and I bear a grudge like a member of the Mafia."

"Is the Mafia a religion?" She is now in question mode, like a trained quiz girl.

"Not specifically. It's more like a tribe."

"Are you and the magician part of the same tribe?"

"Yes, we are," says the magician suddenly and honestly.

"Good heavens, dear. A burst of political solidarity from you? You always said that we were a complete waste of time as a tribe. I shall have to sit down on that rock."

"I can change my mind, can't I?"

"Never too late."

We sit down, looking at the mountains and the sea from a slightly altered perspective. The magician turns his back. He is put out by the sharpness of my tone. I curl my arm around him and Miranda climbs onto my knee. She is tired. Her legs hurt. She's hungry. She wants a drink. When can we go home? As we start down the hill again I catch the magician's eye. "I'm glad you've changed your mind."

We turn off the motorway by the entrance to Auchan. The heat closes over us like a damp blanket as we descend into the valley. The air whistles clammily into the car. Miranda and the magician, fortified by Oranginas, sit side by side in the front, dressed like hoods on summer holidays in their dark glasses and straw hats. I stretch my legs out along the back seat and undo the tighter buttons. Then at the same moment we all see the lights, hear the music. Masked by trees, the flashing bulbs reveal a carousel, rising and falling, the Dodgems clashing on the rink, women screaming and clutching at their skirts as the Big Wheel lurches into the curve, sudden bangs from the shooting galleries. I smell the popcorn, candy floss and poisonous sweets. Toffee apples. Do the French do toffee apples? Can we stop? The magician has already swept dangerously across two lanes and is mounting the kerb. Miranda has suddenly recovered all her energy and is negotiating a budget with the magician for rides, coconut shies if there are any, shooting ducks or rubber rings around piles of presents, at least one go on the Walzer, extra supplements for the Dodgems.

"I just love the Dodgems," she explains. "At the moment my guardian's got me on thirty francs a day, which includes snacks, but not main meals. The fair could be extra, couldn't it? You see, if you pay for three goes on the Dodgems all at once you get one go free and that works out at extra long with a reduction in price. So it's cheaper, isn't it?"

"No it isn't," argues the magician, "it's more expensive. It only works out cheaper if you were going to have three different rides at different times."

Sulk. Miranda hasn't followed his argument, but then, neither have I. Time to enter the negotiations.

"Let's walk round first and then I'll treat you both to Dodgems. Watch your pockets, dears. My eyes can't be everywhere."

Miranda tightens her money belt and looks fierce.

The fair is a surface of changing lights, a code, like an airliner's control panel. Even in the evening sunshine it carries the charge of night. The fair people are night people; bored, watchful, like bouncers in a cut-rate casino. Their hands smell of oil and worn metal instruments, they operate through tokens and cash only. Their profession has the tingle of insanity. It is a very curious thing to do; managing the milder forms of gambling, ghost trains and the pretence of fear, jet cars, creating the illusion of speed and danger, losing your licence if the danger ceases to be illusory. The fair has always been the symbol of corruption and bankrupt illusions. Freaks and beauties, cheating sex, a mini-bordello in the tunnels of love where the sexually titillated can retreat for a smooch, rewards won that dissolve into trash as day comes. I look carefully at the fair. Tangled chains of lights, many bulbs gone, one carousel horse sports a missing leg, sheared off at the knee, the other leg bent and prancing, paint peeling from the Walzer's chariots, cheap toys on plinths, waiting to be won if you can hit a battered row of moving ducks that are so worn they can barely hold their own on the chain. Men and women scratching a living in a poor *quartier*, untouched by the social security system. All vanity has long since departed. Nevertheless, I turn to the magician and snarl, for the sake of that long tradition of moralists, "Thou lookst like Anti-Christ in that lewd hat."

"Have you gone quite mad?" he says.

Miranda decides to lash out on three darts. We line up at the stall. The old woman with green and yellow hair decorated by an enormous polka-dot bow peers at us for a moment. We look as strange as she does.

"*Alors, la moufflette . . .*" She leers at Miranda, who snatches up the darts.

"Take your time, Miranda. Concentrate," I advise.

"Let me do it my way," she says.

The first dart hits the cork backdrop, an extensive necessity for the very inaccurate. The second one strikes the metal edge of the dartboard and falls to the ground. The third is in the green zone, no score.

"*Dommage. Encore une fois . . .*" suggests the witch, putting out her hand for the next ten franc piece.

"*D'accord.*" Miranda filches another coin from the magician, narrows her eyes and lifts her first dart.

"Look only at the red core," says the magician softly, "nothing else."

The first dart hurtles into the centre of the red. I cheer. Miranda grins. Even the witch is impressed.

I let the colours loose to amuse myself. We all hear a faint roll of drums. The witch looks around. The magician sees a naked lady presenting the dartboard dramatically to a vast circus audience and swings round to glare at me.

"Don't cheat. Keep them quiet," he says sharply, but in English. The witch has not understood him and gazes expectantly at the dartboard.

Miranda hits the red again.

"Yes! Yes! *Attention à la troisième!*" We all lean over the counter. Miranda gives me her hat to hold. She assumes a mean expression. And hurls the dart.

Red. Sliced neatly into zones by three darts. Miranda leaps up and down, shrieking.

"Were you helping her?" I demand of the magician.

"No. I swear. I'm so out of practice I don't know that I'd have got it right. She did that on her own."

But the witch suspects us. My hair is too long, my face too wrinkled, my eyes too sharp. I look too much like her.

Miranda has won two goldfish in a large, transparent plastic bowl. She puts her arms around the globe and the fish mouth the walls, puzzled and bored. We then have a long discussion as to whether we should carry them around or take them back to the car. I thank the witch, who is still looking at us suspiciously. She is not convinced that we are genuine. She is a subtle old woman.

"Let's go on one of the rides," suggests the magician.

"But don't you want to win something at the shooting gallery?" Miranda asks. We stand opposite a row of fat thugs who are busy shooting at imitation pigeons.

"We can't play," declares the magician.

"Why not?"

"People think we're cheating because we always win," I explain candidly.

"We are," the magician says gloomily.

"Oh, go on. Show me." Miranda is fascinated.

The magician relents and waits in the queue for a rifle. Miranda hands me the goldfish and then takes up her post next to him. The stall minder tweaks her ear and she recoils at once. Most children hate being touched and adults have an irresistible urge to twiddle, fondle and interfere. I can see that she is thinking about biting his hand. The magician pays for three shots.

His turn.

Three neat, exact explosions and three pigeons flop over

one after the other, all struck at exactly the same point on their anatomy.

"*Alors, vous êtes dans l'armée?*" The keeper's chins vibrate slightly.

"*Non. Dans un orchestre. Même truc,*" says the magician amiably and chooses a modest tin of sweets. We push off at once, both knowing how fatal it is to outstay our welcome.

"Can I have one of the bonbons? And pleeeeeease let's try another stall?"

Miranda has spotted a certain winning streak and is contemplating becoming the magician's manager.

"No," we both chant in chorus.

"But I didn't know you were a practised sniper," I hear her lament above the solid sucking of the bonbon that she has between her teeth. "We could win millions . . ."

"Finish that before you go on the Dodgems," I advise, "or you'll bang into someone, swallow it and choke to death."

She sucks in her teeth and takes back the goldfish bowl, which she carries in triumph.

We look round the sideshows, resisting a tattooed lady and a real python coiled round an Arab, both of whom, the magician asserts, will be devastatingly underpaid. We put five francs into a machine full of trinkets and I win a small black plastic rat with red eyes. Miranda takes it over, going all sentimental because it reminds her of Lucy, who is being looked after in London by her real grandmother. Why can't we bring her on holiday? I don't fancy going through British customs with a pet black rat and no import licence. The crowds are increasing. Children push past us. The air smells of oil, sweat and sugar, the music dazzles our ears.

They are playing old Elvis hits at the Dodgems. We hover on the brink, waiting for two free cars. I buy a handful of tokens from a sulky-looking boy with huge gold earrings and take back the goldfish. Miranda and the magician can have a car each so that she has someone to chase and bang into. They both adjust their hats and dark glasses. Will the magician's length fit into one of the Dodgems? Some doubt is expressed. I refuse to participate on the grounds that my false teeth will fly out.

What Miranda and the magician both love about the Dodgems is the irresponsibility; being able to crash into whoever you damn well like with no harm done. Amid the roar of "Jailhouse Rock" the sparkling cars cruise to a standstill. Like divers poised on the edge of a pool, they lean out, the magician expectant and attenuated, waiting to grab a free car. Two giggling girls climb out of the tiny seats in a flurry of knickers and stocking tops. Thirty years ago we all used to wear tights with short skirts. And forty years ago we wore bobby socks to jive. When did stockings come back into fashion? I stand staring, feeling my age. The magician leaps. I can hear him shouting.

"That one, Miranda. The red one. I'll get the green."

He slides across the polished metal and stuffs his legs down beside the wheel. He now looks like a stick insect, ready to pounce. Miranda has her hat pulled low. Her getaway car is poised to swerve away from the kerb as soon as the signal is given. The signal is "Blue Suede Shoes". In a halo of blue sparks they whirl off *en masse*.

The French drive no differently on the roads. I watch horrified at some near misses and direct hits. Miranda and the magician are chasing each other. They are both very good at gaining speed on the open outer circle and then spinning swiftly in for the kill. The magician bumps her twice running.

"No cheating!" she shouts, suspecting him of using the same strategies for accuracy that brought such success in the shooting gallery. Miranda is a very bad loser. Bang! She scores a hit as he is caught behind a family car of Papa and shrieking infant.

"Keep score!" she yells at me as she whirls past.

The two of them are so fast and so accurate that they begin to attract attention. They don't look at all like a father and daughter. The magician is timeless, but old, like a vampire still in service. Miranda does not look French. She is too blonde, too powerful, and she isn't wearing little jewelled earrings. What marks them out are the dark glasses, which turn the rink into a sinister, luminous zone of crashing colours and torrents of sparks, and the extraordinarily silly hats. KISS ME QUICK and SUGAR MOON in fluorescent letters like mad political slogans. Onlookers begin to cheer as the score mounts. The other participants in the chariot race become collaborators, shouting:

"*Attention! Elle est derrière!*"

"*PAF! Gagné!*"

"*Vite, SUGAR, vite! Par ici!*"

"*Bien bloqué!*"

"*Vas-y! Je te suive!*"

A community of crashing Dodgems begins to form on the rink. Pleasure, excitement and laughter are infectious. The human race is addicted to spectacle. They will gather to watch anything that is boisterous or noisy, always in the hope of seeing blood. Market vendors and auctioneers know this. Promises of gain and loss need to be sharpened by tears and pain. All the shouting, clapping public that has gathered around the rink is secretly hoping for squashed hands, pinched feet, whiplash and wailing. We watch the Big Wheel turn, longing to see someone fall out.

I am so engrossed in the performance that I do not notice the sudden cold on my back in the hot night. The trickle of sweat, glacial against my neck, stops me in the middle of my gestures. The music, noise, clapping, vanish as if the plug has been pulled out at the mains. In the absolute, suspended silence I put the goldfish carefully down on the ground and turn, terrified, to confront whoever is standing behind me. My hand shakes. I steady my glasses on my nose. At first my eyes are too clouded to see. The terrible cold forms a capsule around me. I have been plucked out of time.

Standing in front of me, their faces grave and steady, are an

Englishwoman in her forties, petite with narrow shoulders, wearing a blue linen suit and a long string of pearls. Beside her, with a hand on her shoulder, is a tall Arab woman dressed like a nomad from the desert, in heavy, beaded robes. They do not smile or offer any sign of recognition. They do not speak. How can two faces, so familiar and so loved, appear uncanny and menacing? For the first time that I can remember, I am pierced through by the fear of death. I will no longer choose, act, decide, or judge for myself. I will no longer see this world, this world of music, of life, of physical sensations. I will no longer work or eat or wake. I will never laugh with Miranda again, never hold the magician in my arms. I will no longer be. Of what consequence is it that I am old, toothless, tired and fragile? I still am. The great gulf of not-being opens before me. If we are naïve we fear death in terms of sensation. It is much more terrifying not to feel, and therefore not to be.

The ghosts stand before me, passive and knowing. They are confirming my most appalling fears. I can neither move nor speak. There is no escape, no evasion, no reprieve. I stand inside the moment where "we all must die" becomes – I must die – and soon.

With a thundercrash the music begins again. The two women vanish. Nothing remains in the dusk but the doubtful glimmer of a firefly and the sweat chilly on the inside of my shirt. I wipe my face carefully. My knees are shaking. The goldfish circulate stupidly between my ankles. The Dodgems thunder past and Elvis rocks on into eternity. The people around me, shouting, clapping, cheering, have noticed nothing.

It is quite dark before Miranda and the magician can be prised away from the Dodgems. Their stomachs are demanding Coke and pizza. The magician loves junk food. Years travelling in other countries with his orchestra have ensured a cast-iron stomach and a taste for anything made in the USA.

"Make sure she eats decent food occasionally," I say ruefully, paying for an evil-looking cheese and tomato pizza, which, with some difficulty, they cut into two.

"Have a pâté sandwich," suggests the magician, "and sit down. You're looking a bit peculiar. But I suppose it could be the lights."

He and Mirånda settle themselves into the plastic chairs at the makeshift outdoor café and munch contentedly on their E-numbers with their added artificial colouring. I find that the decision to say nothing has already been made for me. I clutch the goldfish for comfort.

"It's eleven o'clock. Shall we go home to the hotel?" This is my suggestion.

"Oh, please, one more ride," begs Miranda. "Can we go on the Big Wheel?"

"You haven't had your Latin lesson today, young lady."

"Oh, pleeease."

"And you were up late last night. And you haven't had a siesta."

But the magician seconds her. "Just once on the Big Wheel. Then we'll put the goldfish to bed."

"Where?" she demands.

"In the bath for tonight. And we'll buy a fish tank with an oxygen pump at the *quincaillerie* tomorrow," he promises.

We knock back the Coke and head for the Big Wheel.

This costs an astonishing thirty francs each. I look at the antique mechanical structure, which should be on sale at Sotheby's and decide that it must be danger money, so that they can cope with their insurance. A fabulous view of the city lights is promised at the top of the curve. I renounce the pleasure, this time pleading vertigo. And I send them up, up, up, into the endless orange night. Miranda accepts the magician's arm and holds on tight. I overhear him assuring her of his ability to fly as the wheel jerks free of the earth. Fortune's queen, I watch Miranda's multicoloured lurex cycling shorts and Clarks sandals disappearing above my head. I stand back. I do not feel at all philosophical; but I am more at ease with myself. After all, it is by no means certain that, in death, I will simply inhabit a terrifying, chilly silence. It is perfectly possible that eternal peace will be sufficiently rich and interesting to meet all my needs. It may be that I shall not care one way or another. I calm myself with platitudes. Death may well be an experience beyond all our anxious imaginings. A warm voice sings in my ear. "The Kingdom of Heaven is like unto a ferris wheel . . ." And shall I become part of the eternal return? The food chain? The supposedly everlasting cycle of rebirth, life, death, renewed life? For which there is precious little evidence? Time is singular, linear, apocalyptic. All history is caught in that flood rushing towards the precipice. For a moment I dawdle in the shallows, caught in an eddy of my own reflections. Naught we know dies. Another one of the Great Lies by which we manage our existence. Everything dies, rests locked in the handsome family vault of death, the chambers of non-being. Where there is room for all, and then for more.

Miranda and the magician surge past me, waving and screaming. I watch them rise, buoyant, joyful and charged with pure verve and gusto. As the wheel turns they soar out into space, so confident now that they are making the swing rock backwards and forwards, so that the world tips beneath their feet. Before them I see the vast plains of boundless day.

And my fear drops away. I know that I am no longer facing my death alone. I am casting off, sailing away from the limits of the shore's edge, surrounded by my own people. I lean out into the warm dark and wave wildly at the two of them, high above me, riding the night sky. When the wheel stops the magician clambers out and rushes towards me, catching me in his arms.

"What's the matter with you? Were you frightened?" I stand there laughing, clutching the goldfish bowl.

"No, no," he stammers quickly, "but something's gone funny in my head. As we were coming down I saw you standing there, waving. And I saw, I swear it, one on each side, Cynthia and Fatima, both of them, laughing and laughing."

"Hush," I say, putting a finger on his lips, "here comes Miranda."

We creep into the hotel well after midnight, the magician wearing his dark glasses, hat down, collar up. Back in the world of the wealthy middle classes we must expect recognition and persecution. Miranda is clutching the goldfish. But the manager is waiting at the desk, watchful as Cerberus.

"Ah, Monsieur!" He launches himself at the magician, "There is a very urgent phone message for you. And a FAX. From Paris. I was asked to notify you at once."

He stops and bows discreetly.

"*Merde!*" mutters the magician, glancing down at the FAX, which is written in French.

"What is it?" Miranda asks before I can. We both peer at the FAX which appears to be translated from the Arabic.

"It's from Gilles. You remember Gilles. Yes, you do. I'm as good as married to him."

"Oh, Gilles. Handsome, charming Gilles. Your agent. How did he know you were here?"

"He's worse than a wife. Or a jealous husband for that matter. All my movements are always accounted for. He knows where I am every minute of the day. Look, he's even got the hotel's bloody FAX number." The magician is shouting. "He'd be on the phone if it wasn't after midnight."

The manager has at last understood a few words of the magician's tirade.

"Ah, yes. The Monsieur asked you to ring him if you were home before twelve."

"You see," rages the magician.

"But what's it about?" I persist.

"Gilles is coming down tomorrow. He'll be here by lunchtime. Slovnic's been taken ill. He was playing at the Centre Culturel tomorrow night. Gilles wants me to step in and replace him. Seeing as how I'm already here." He adds bitterly, "For twice the fee. He just wants his bloody percentage."

"Can you do it? What's on the programme?" I ask practically.

"Do it? Of course I can bloody well do it. Mozart. Nothing but effing Mozart. I played nothing but Mozart all last year for the bi-centenary. And if I have to tramp through another one of those fucking piano concertos, I'll . . ."

Miranda is loving this.

"Thank you very much," I smile at the manager, who is standing there, bowing at the magician's bad language like a marionette. I propel the enraged magician towards the lift.

"I thought Mozart was good," says Miranda.

"He is good," shouts the magician, "but I've played thirty-five concerts . . ."

"Shhhhhhh, shhhhhh, shhhhhh . . . we'll think about it all tomorrow morning."

"Gilles will be on the phone by seven."

"And take off that hat. While you were ranting at the manager he was busy deciphering the slogan on your head. Which still says KISS ME QUICK."

"I've started wishing that Verdi had written piano concertos," the magician wails in despair.

"Didn't he?" Miranda is pretending to press all the buttons in the lift, including those marked SOUS-SOL.

"No he didn't. He wrote operas. And the odd requiem."

"Are they good?"

"Yes. Very. I'll take you to one."

"Miranda. Pick up those goldfish and fill the bath while you're cleaning your teeth. Make sure the plug holds. Cold water, mind."

We arrive at our floor. As the lift doors open I lean back against the red velvet lining of the interior, content, and very, very, tired. Cynthia's perfume fills the corridor. The scent is no longer sinister and I breathe her presence, reassured.

*

Sure enough, the phone rings at seven. It is on my side of the bed. I surface blurred, like a fading photograph. It is the young woman in reception and she is dreadfully embarrassed. She begins to splutter.

"*Excusez-moi... c'est un appel pour Monsieur... Un appel urgent de la part de son collègue à Paris... et il n'est pas dans sa chambre... Excusez-moi, mais c'est le monsieur à Paris qui a insisté...*" She gives up in a series of gulps.

The magician wakes up, takes the pillow off his head and snatches the phone.

"*Ecoutez... oui, passez-moi ce monsieur vite. Gilles! Ouais, ouais bien sûr, c'est moi. Qu'est ce que t'as fait? Mais si, je suis en vacances... j'ai aucun engagement avant mi-Septembre... Mais si, je t'ai dit...*"

Vacances. That's a new name for it. I settle down on the bolster like a martyred knight and put both the magician's pillow and mine over my face. The light batters at the slats on the shutters, but the morning air still smells fresh and cold. The curling phone wire begins to give me the sensation of being garrotted. I look down at my stomach which makes a large mound in the bed. I let the torrent of irritated, but excited French pass over me. The magician rattles into the phone like a gatling gun shedding its load. Ah, the great mystery of complete coherence at seven in the morning. Miranda and I never speak until ten o'clock when we are on holiday, beyond an articulate and expressive sequence of nods and grunts.

"*... oui, oui, écoute, tu prends un taxi... mais, oui... ouf! mais toujours Mozart, tu sais, j'en ai marre... bon, je te pardonne... à plus tard... allez... ciao.*"

Bang.

A giant wriggle and then he lies still, thinking. I can feel him moving into the memory of the music he will play tonight. Suddenly he pats my arm.

"*Mon amour.* We must go and look at the Steinway in the Centre Culturel. I haven't played there for four years. It may be a different piano. And I can't remember the size of the hall . . ."

"*Café*," I murmur, feebly.

The magician snatches up the phone again and orders breakfast for two, in my room, but on his bill. I sit up, impressed by his shamelessness.

"The hotel gossip will be electrifying."

"Bullshit!" he snaps. "There was that profile about us in *L'Evénement du jeudi* three years ago. With ghastly photographs of you. Everybody knows."

"Then why am I never recognized?"

"Because you're always incognito. Anyway, you never look the same two months running."

"I remember that article. Didn't they use some awful queer formula like close companions or life-long friends? Miranda cut out all the pictures. She'd never seen you before. Were we still speaking then? Or was that during a rupture?"

"Oh, God knows. Where's your dressing gown? I want to piss. Do you and Miranda have a secret code about who gets to use the bathroom?"

"Yes, if her door is closed I can go. But she's asleep. Don't wake her up."

I hear the magician cleaning his teeth. He must be using my electric toothbrush. He comes back humming. Gilles was the bringer of good news. The piano concerto is No 20 in D Minor, K 466.

"Which I haven't played since I last recorded it with the Berlin Philharmonic."

"I don't know how you tell them apart." I sit up unsteadily.

The magician bangs open the shutters and strides up and down the balcony, looking out at the sea. Amazingly, he begins to fiddle with the electric blind, making it fold and unfold like a bowing flunkey.

"Don't. You'll break it," I say in exactly the same tones I used for Miranda. And just like her, he makes a face, insists on doing it one more time to defy me and then decides to leave it up. I stagger off to the bathroom. Someone knocks on the door.

"I'll get it." The magician flings both sides wide open, in a convincing imitation of Vincent Price, and behold, there is the manager, bowing, apologizing and presenting our *thé citron*, coffee and warm fresh rolls wrapped in white linen, *confiture d'abricots* in a crystal dish, tiny packets of Président butter. He has taken upon himself the honour of serving us personally, trusting that everything is to Monsieur's satisfaction. I emerge from the bathroom in a pink cloud of dignity and ask him to assist with a little problem. I am unable to take my bath. The magician sweeps off to the balcony with the tray and the manager oozes his way into the cavern of scents and towels. Two fat sleek goldfish are circulating calmly in the tub. The unfortunate manager retreats, bristling with instructions on size of tank, oxygen pumps and maidenhair weeds. For the first and last time I have openly taken advantage of the magician's fame to get something done. Chuckling at my performance, the magician calls to the disappearing manager to put the fish tank on his bill.

So this is the beginning of the last day. I am delighted by my own placid sense of continuity. By eight-thirty the tank is plugged in and bubbling at my feet and I am trying to catch the goldfish in my tooth mug. They slide past, glittering and elastic. Miranda appears, nodding sleepily, and strolls into the bathroom. She yawns approval at the apparition of the fish tank, then walks out on to the balcony, gives the magician a hug, puts her finger in the apricot jam, hooks out an entire sugary apricot and swallows it down.

"Can we go to the beach today?"

"I'm committed to Mozart."

"All day?"

"There'll be a rehearsal at some point."

"Well, can you come to the beach before or after your

rehearsal? We will go to the beach, won't we?" She shouts for me.

"Yes, my dear, we will. Now come and catch this goldfish. I've done my duty and caught one. They're your responsibility. You won them."

"Can we take goldfish through the British customs or will they demand an import licence?" asks the magician gloomily.

"That, my love, is your problem." I am unashamedly, irresponsibly pleased. The telephone rings again. "Answer it, dear. It's sure to be for you."

And it is. The young Englishman who is to conduct the concert has at last caught up with the magician. They have never played together or even met before. The young conductor is a rising star, but he is overwhelmed by fame. I hear the magician being very foreign for effect, and remorselessly professional.

We divide our forces in the morning heat. The modern Centre Culturel is installed inside a huge nineteenth-century theatre with fake Greek columns and vast portico. The magician enlists me in support. Miranda holds court upon the beach, supervised by Mrs Pink Nipples, who, this morning, is decked out in a striped bikini with a swaying fringe. I dispense suncream, hats, packets of biscuits, bottles of Badoit and instructions. The magician descends from the promenade to shake hands with her. As he takes off his undertaker's black hat, she recognizes him.

"*Excusez-moi . . . mais je vous connais. Vous êtes . . .*" He bows. She is thrilled. Apparently the Centre Culturel has been galvanized by the prospect of a complete sell-out and the promise of television. The magician's gaunt face has appeared on posters everywhere in the centre of the city with a large yellow headline.

CE SOIR: CENTRE CULTUREL
HOMMAGE A MOZART 20H30

The ticket prices have doubled. We also discover that the

obsequious hotel manager is no fool. He has sent forth minions to purchase a block booking of expensive seats on behalf of the hotel, which his clients may order at reception and have added to their bill. There is already a waiting list for returns. The chambermaid reveals, smiling at me cheekily, that she has been offered considerable sums for a quick, private inspection of our rooms. I hand her 500 francs to keep the Great French Public out. There is also considerable speculation concerning Miranda's identity. She must be somebody's granddaughter. But whose?

The press are waiting on the steps of the Centre Culturel, with a cameraman from FRANCE 2. I put on my dark glasses and look round for a dark alleyway.

"Oh, no you don't." The magician's fingers are clamped round my wrist. "Just keep your glasses on and don't answer any of their questions."

We march up the steps like visiting royalty. The magician becomes a distinguished public man in a matter of seconds and makes intelligent comments about Mozart. I try to look like a visiting Mafia boss to intimidate the journalists. But inevitably, one of them is fearless and has done her research. She addresses me directly, using one of my names that is seldom published in the press, and asks me about my long association with the magician and the influence of my radical *prises de positions* on political issues. Suddenly bloody-minded, I point out that the magician has done a great deal to liberate a revolutionary string quartet from the clutches of a South American general after they had been imprisoned for playing Beethoven in memory of the "disappeared".

" . . . which was a matter that he brought to my attention," I say firmly, "rather than the other way round."

There is a surge of questions about politics and music and we retreat up the steps, giving them one last photo opportunity, before they can attack the personal angle. The young British conductor is waiting inside the swing doors. He is small, curly-headed and terrified. The magician looks him

over carefully. Then smiles. We proceed to the concert hall.
The orchestra are bored and mutinous. They are fiddling with
their instruments. The cellists are smoking. Yet they all rise
to their feet when the magician's tall, strange figure approaches
them, soundlessly descending the smooth red flow of carpet.
They rise to their feet to applaud him. He greets them peacefully, shakes hands with the leader of the orchestra, kisses the
timpanist, who is an old friend, then sits down quietly at
the piano and waits. He is concentrating on the keys, but
there is no trembling tic at the corner of his eyes. The young
conductor leans over the piano to consult with him. He listens,
nods, but does not speak.

I have watched him play so many times. Each time is
different. He is extraordinary because of his apparent complicity with the music. Each time he plays not only as if he
has never played that piece before, but as if no one else has
ever done so either. There is an intimacy and an edge in his
performances, an element of risk. Breathlessness seizes the
audience, even the musicians. Orchestras are usually full of
cynical, difficult people. But, playing with the magician, many
of them remember why they first learned that instrument, first
heard and loved that particular composer, first fell in love. He
unlocks their desires and transforms their memories into
music. He carries them before him. They play like giants.

The magician attracts cranks and lunatics, people who hear
voices and see visions. Old ladies spend their pensions on his
concerts, young men dream he is their master; he receives
letters from prisons, from missions in jungles, from archae-
ologists on expeditions, from boarding schools, from
monasteries, from hospitals, from China. He commands
unbelievable fees.

They play the concerto straight through from beginning to
end without a pause. Am I dreaming? The auditorium has
apparently filled up around me. There are young people in
shorts, T-shirts and jeans – silently taking up their places like
the children of Hamelin. No – here is a famous face, a woman

I know is slipping into the seat beside me, kissing me on the cheek, but never speaking or taking her eyes off the magician. She is a black American soprano, ample, powerful, outspoken. She squeezes my hand and then settles into the shape of the Allegro. As the magician draws a fine, steady, concluding line beneath the last notes a thunderous crescendo of applause greets his ageless face, blurred, raised at last from the subsiding row of black and white keys. I am not alone. There are one hundred and fifty people around me, standing, applauding, acknowledging the real magician. The soprano takes my hand again; she is all caring anxiety. I find that there are tears on my cheeks.

It is one of those Mozart concerts you can only afford to put on in the provinces, where there are amateur choirs prepared to give up all the hours God made for no money at all. The overture from *Don Giovanni*, the Piano Concerto No 20 in D Minor, interval – and then the C Minor Mass. Miranda is suffering from sunburn on her shoulders and she is too hot. She wriggles beside me and complains. I send her off for an iced drink. She returns at once, tearful and furious. One of the photographers haunting the bar startled her with the suddenness of his flash, and took a picture without asking. I stride off to the bar, murderous. I can see the hovering reptiles, but of course I pass unrecognized. Confrontation seems useless, so I simply buy the iced drink myself and go back to our box.

"What did you do to them?" asks Miranda gleefully.

"Gave them indigestion for the rest of the evening," I say mildly and sink down into red velvet. Miranda sucks her ice cubes and swings her feet, very pleased.

The magician appears beside us just before the performance begins. He looks magnificent in white tie and tails which Gilles carried all the way down from Paris on the TGV, on the grounds that nobody in the Midi could possibly be as tall as the magician.

"Watch out for the paparazzi," I warn him, "they got Miranda in the bar."

"Good for you, Sugar. You'll be all over the *Midi Libre* tomorrow morning," he says easily, nicking one of her ice cubes. He turns to me. "Gilles is selling them stories of secret marriages to explain Miranda."

"You're too old to be my dad," she says cheekily.

"My dear, I'm being passed off as your grandfather. An old wolf like me. Eyebrows have gone up all over Neuilly and Gilles is loving every moment. His mobile phone hasn't stopped ringing since he got here. I wouldn't put it past him to be upping my fees at this very moment."

"Can I have a go on his mobile phone?" Miranda loves technology. "Why haven't you got one?"

"What an idea. I'd hate it. I don't do that kind of job. It's useful for Gilles. He carries his office around with him. He's been chatting up the conductor, who he swears is in love with me."

"Really? Is he?" Miranda is fascinated. I glare at the magician who shrugs guiltily, kisses us both and slips off.

"Is he very good? Like you say?" Miranda asks anxiously as the leader of the orchestra arrives to huge applause. The house is sold out and Miranda wants the magician to win. "I mean really truly good. Cynthia and Fatima said he was."

"Yes. He really truly is. The best." I reassure her. "Just listen. You'll see."

And she does.

The magician plays three encores before they will let him go. We fight our way into his dressing-room, which he is sharing with the American soprano. Miranda gazes at her admiringly and she produces cold bottles of Orangina from a travelling ice box. The magician changes into an anonymous black shirt and jeans. We all slip back to the box during the Kyrie Eleison when the houselights have dimmed a little and sail through the C Minor Mass in a burst of Hallelujahs.

Gilles has thought of everything. There is a taxi waiting

by the back door. We slink out like wanted criminals, our heads down. I assure the magician that the press will be lying pissed in the bar. They loathe serious music and no one takes photographs after a performance when the stars all look ancient and mortal without their robes and make up. But of course we have not counted on the hotel.

The hotel is *en fête*. As we arrive in the taxi I realize that a crowd, headed by the entrepreneurial manager, the Mayor of the city, his wife, their official photographer, selected members of the Conseil Général, the guests who got into the concert, those that didn't and are still furious, Sven and his friend with shaved head and tattoos, the *maître d'hôtel* and all his staff, my chambermaid and an array of dogs, are all cheering beneath a string of Japanese lanterns and waiting to greet us.

"What do we do? Drive on?" I ask the magician.

But Miranda is already climbing out of the taxi. She has seen Josette and Delphine, who are waving frantically from the top of the steps and shouting, Miranda, Miranda. They are under the impression that she is the Infant Prodigy and has just played the piano before millions of people. The wonderful Pink Nipples are encased in an evening gown and she claims my acquaintance like an old friend. I hand her to the magician and he arranges us carefully, one on each arm. We sweep into the hotel, the children bounding before us.

The dining-room has been organized for an impromptu reception. The Mayor makes a speech. There must be an election pending. We shake a great many outstretched hands. They beg the magician to play for them again. But the only available piano is hidden in a corner of the ballroom, where we once danced the tango, and which has now been transformed into the gymnasium and aerobics club. The magician raises his hands for silence. The French are incapable of being so, but he reduces them to mutters and rustles. He speaks in French.

"I can't make speeches. And I've made enough music for

tonight. But I will thank you for this generous reception by doing something I love to do. Making magic. It's a little-known fact about me that I don't only play the piano, but that I am a real magician."

The dining-room erupts with surprise, applause and delight. They would have wilted reverentially before any more Mozart.

The magician sends his three apprentices off upstairs to bring down his equipment as we rearrange the room according to his directions. A fresh white tablecloth covers his table.

Miranda is breathless and glowing.

"We found all this. Look. Laid out on your bed. Like it was all prepared."

She produces a spangled box, sinister and very light, a top hat, a pair of white silk gloves and a purple feather boa, which is draped over the shoulders of all three children like an elongated floral snake. They gather round the magician with their elbows on the table, desperate not to miss a single moment. He does not send them away. He puts on his top hat and gloves and as he does so we begin to hear the circus music, the distant ferocity of a pianola, pounding out the formulas for excitement. The light shimmers from the Japanese lanterns and the room is very hot. We titter and giggle like children, passionately longing to be entertained, all believers in the magician's art. Only his face and his bright white gloves stand out in the marvellous darkness.

Then he begins.

Out of the box come a sequence of enormous silk scarves, orange, pink, emerald green, cobalt blue. He knots them swiftly into a long thin comet's tail, encircles the delighted children with colour, then flicks the scarves back one after another, into his gloved hand. They vanish without trace. Amid our wild, infantile applause, Miranda inspects his sleeves suspiciously. There is nothing there.

He reaches into her ear. What's this? An egg. A real egg.

And Delphine has one on her shoulder. Josette is hiding a huge brown egg in the pocket of her smock. Lest we suspect them of being his accomplices the magician advances on the audience. Mrs Pink Nipples, grandly seated on my right hand, has all the scarves, no longer knotted, one after another, pouring from the sleeve of her gown. She screams with pleasure and stands up in a torrent of scarves. To his horror, Monsieur the Mayor discovers a little white mouse in his dress suit pocket, nibbling the tip of his impeccable starched handkerchief. The official photographer snatches a wonderful picture of the magician relieving him of the uninvited rodent. Out of the top hat leaps a small white rabbit. And then another. There is one for Josette and one for Delphine.

"*Et pour moi?*" cries Miranda.

"No," replies the magician in French, as if the exchange was part of a script, "we really can't take a white rabbit through British customs. And you've already got two goldfish upstairs."

The crowd love this, and cheer, delighted. There is a drum roll in the distance. The magician peers, amazed, into his top hat and out pours a torrent of balloons. They float up amongst the chandeliers and bump against the curtain pelmets – one or two escape out on to the terrace. The feather boa, suddenly animate, uncoils on the table, surges around the squealing children before settling contentedly upon the magician's shoulders. We field the torrent of balloons, drunk with excitement. The magician peers into his hat, out of which he draws an umbrella, a kettle, a frying pan, a walking stick, a tennis racquet, rigid in its press, a pair of binoculars, a cordless telephone which rings as he holds it up, and a large pot of honey. Laughing, he distributes this peculiar, incoherent collection of objects to members of the audience. Sven opens the umbrella, incredulous. It is large, solid, real. A British golfing umbrella with a folding seat. The kettle has a French plug, already attached. The audience cheers wildly. In the shouting excitement I hear him say softly to Miranda, "Now this is very special. You must give this to your guardian, my dear. To keep safely."

The small phial with the cork stopper is of smoky blue Venetian glass. It is warm to the touch, as if the contents were smouldering. Carefully keeping it level, Miranda brings it to me, her cheeks glowing with sunburn. Never has death sent so innocent and charming a messenger.

I gaze at the man I have passionately loved for over forty years. He bows. He has played his part. The gesture is immaculate, elegant, a joker's trick carried out before his public, a perfect folding of white gloves.

Now he is gazing back into his top hat as Miranda leaps towards him. As if surprised, he reels backwards, the hat falls to the table and out of it pours a flock of white doves, dozens of them, swirling out through the open windows and away into the night. The magician has the children in his arms, the top hat once more upon his head, bowing and smiling at our assembled excitement. The audience is on its feet for him once more. The music reaches a crescendo of cymbals and brass. The performance is over.

Afterwards, we sit peacefully on the terrace, drinking champagne at one in the morning. The crowds have ebbed. The magician sits beside me. Suddenly, he says, "Listen. I'm worried about Miranda. Will I manage? Can I give her all the comfort and happiness you did? Will her parents have confidence in me?"

"My dear, I don't think you have quite realized who Miranda is. She's in the doorway. Look."

Miranda is loving the attention. Josette and Delphine think that she is already famous and are hanging on her every word. Well, perhaps she is. She knows that we are watching. And in the light of the Japanese lanterns as she turns to wave, the magician sees her as if for the first time. She stands in the doorway, an eleven-year-old English schoolgirl, on the threshold of her life as a woman, yet also the child of magic and darkness. The black rat is perched on her shoulder, its naked tail pink and obscene in the flickering lights. Two small bats, furry and rapid, circle her head in the thick summer night. She smiles, waves and turns away. All the monsters of darkness are prepared to obey her. Miranda will be our inheritor.

I smile calmly at the magician. "No harm will come to you. I will watch over you always. You have my word."

We walk on the terrace among the towering bougainvillaeas and pots of geraniums. I sense the glass phial warm in my pocket. I hear Cynthia's laughter, long before I see the glow of Fatima's dancing fireflies, glimmering through the wisteria in the scented gloom.

"Goodbye, my dear," I say to the magician and set off down the steps into the dark.

Praise for **Hallucinating Foucault**

"If you buy one book this week, make it *Hallucinating Foucault* . . . this novel leaves you perspiring, but chillingly inspired."
The Observer

". . . a magnificently wrought tale of obsession, madness and sexuality that does an imaginative justice to Foucault's own themes. . . . Duncker has brought complex critical ideas into the realms of drama – and love. As such, this is a compelling *tour de force* lit with both passion and verve."
New Statesman and Society

". . . a challenging, provocative first novel . . . *Hallucinating Foucault* is cunning, post-modern . . . but one ends up believing in Duncker as a novelist for the simple, old-fashioned reason that she has made us believe in her seething, wounded creation."
The Independent

"Duncker manages her brainy material with a touch so deft it is almost skittish, inserts little hooks into the heart as well as the mind, and rounds the whole lot off with a thriller-like twist."
The Independent on Sunday

"Her images have a memorable brilliance: . . . Her provocative writing is welcome."
Financial Times

"Patricia Duncker's brilliant first novel is an unmitigated delight. Written in spare, incisive prose, *Hallucinating Foucault* is rich with ideas . . . moving and curiously romantic at the same time. Highly recommended."
Gay Times